# DIRECT CONNECT TO GOD

# DIRECT CONNECT TO GOD

## TRUE STORIES OF HOPE, HEALING & MIRACLES

DEBRA MARTIN AND SHERI GETTEN

SEEING VISIONS, VOICING
AND HEARING WORDS FAR
BEYOND HUMAN INSIGHT

Waterside Press

Published by Waterside Press

ISBN 978-1-941768-61-7 print edition
ISBN 978-1-941768-60-0 ebook

"You cannot fail when you walk in God's light." - Debra and Sheri

# DEDICATION

*We dedicate this book to God. We pray that each and every per-son who reads this book will feel love and healing through God's words. We are honored and humbled to be part of God's miracles. With God all things are possible...*

# CONTENTS

# PUBLISHER'S NOTE

Debra Martin and Sheri Getten have developed a healing technique of their own which is not being done anywhere else in the world. They have brought a piece of heaven here for you to read in this book. They are bringing you a direct connect with God. Each healing chapter was transcribed word by word from their healing sessions. No words that came directly from God were taken out or changed. While reading this book, you are connecting to God's frequency and vibration. Through these words from God, allow yourself to open your heart and feel His love, see His visions, and take a spiritual journey to places that most people think are unattainable. You may identify with one or all of the healing chapters.

Debra Martin and Sheri Getten provide the connection to God by being God's instruments to send energy to help the healing process. Some of their clients are also being seen by doctors. These doctors provide their own medical techniques. Debra and Sheri do not claim to be doctors. They always recommend that their clients keep up their medical care, for it all goes hand in hand.

# ACKNOWLEDGMENTS

Susy Smith – Thank you to the deceased Susy Smith for sending Debra an email on September 20, 2013, at 10:24 p.m that dated back to April 2006. Thank you for opening the door to our literary agent, Bill Gladstone. Without you, this book would have never reached his hands.

Bill Gladstone - Thank you for believing and trusting; it is not a coincidence that Susy Smith guided us to you. Thank you for becoming our literary agent.

Anne Puryear & Herb Puryear - We are honored and humbled that Anne and Herb believed in and embraced us with their love. They trusted us, opened their doors, and allowed the healings to begin at their sacred home, The Logos Center located in Scottsdale, Arizona.

We give thanks to The Logos Center for its pureness, holiness, sacredness, and oneness with God.

Thank you to Dr. Eben Alexander, author of *Proof of Heaven*, and Karen Newell, co-founder of Scared Acoustics, for studying our brainwaves during healing sessions.

Jaclyn Vigil – We are truly grateful for the many hours you spent editing and polishing our book to make it come to life.

Ken Fraser at IMPACT bookdesigns.com – We are so grateful for his vision in designing our book cover. We truly believe God worked through him.

We give thanks to all those who have walked with us and believed in our work. We are deeply grateful.

We give thanks to all those who included their stories in this book. We know that each and every person was guided to us through God. God chose each and every one of you to be part of this book. Without you, this book would not have come to life. We believe that through your stories, others will be healed. When one is healed, we are all healed.

"When you trust in thy word, you stand in my name and we are One." - Debra and Sheri

# FOREWORD

We are fortunate to be living in such an exciting time, scientifically speaking.

Although materialism, the assertion that consciousness is produced by and ends with the brain is still the prevailing theory in the vast majority of Western classrooms, laboratories, and surgical suites, it is simply a philosophical viewpoint and only one possible explanation for consciousness. Cutting-edge research continues to demonstrate what great minds like Hippocrates (the father of modern medicine), William James (the father of American psychology), and Max Planck (the father of quantum physics) have always known: Consciousness is merely received and interpreted by the brain and its effects can expand across space and time.

Here are what some other renowned thinkers have had to say on the subject: "Materialism is the greatest superstition of our age... In spite of the complete absence of evidence, the belief that the brain produces consciousness endures and has ossified into dogma... Consciousness can operate beyond the brain, body, and the present, as hundreds of experiments and millions of testimonials affirm."

—physician Larry Dossey

"There is still no proof that life and minds can be explained by physics and chemistry alone."

—biologist Rupert Sheldrake

"The brain does not produce consciousness at all, any more than a television set creates the programs that appear on its screen."

—astronomer David Darling

"The brain breathes mind like the lungs breathe air."

—religious studies scholar Huston Smith

"About all we know about consciousness is that it has something to do with the head, rather than the foot."

—physicist Nick Herbert

For the rare critical thinker who is able to transcend the ideology of materialism and embrace the scientific evidence for the non-local nature of consciousness, phenomena like near-death experiences, telepathy, remote viewing, premonitions, and energy healing are not only possible but expected.

I consider myself one of these critical thinkers and my scientific training is in physiology, so when Debra and Sheri began sharing their reports of energy, or consciousness-based healings with me, I was not surprised by their results. Impressed and curious, yes, but not surprised.

I noticed that there were two main aspects to most, if not all, of the cases Debra described to me: (1) the actual healing (that is, the presence of a health-related problem and then its subsequent absence) and (2) the existence of verifiable facts (for example, accurate information about specific body parts, diagnoses, events, etc.).

Two additional themes that seemed to be present in some but not all of the cases were (3) the existence of predictive information about experiences or events that will happen after the healing takes place and (4) the inclusion of metaphysical explanations for, and/or lessons to be learned from, the ailments or the healing.

I am particularly interested in the metaphysical aspects of disease and know this is an important factor too often ignored in allopathic healthcare. About twenty years ago, I was diagnosed with multiple sclerosis (MS) and I often share publicly the present challenges that diagnosis brings. I have drawn a direct correlation between the disease and certain events, stressors, and psychological components in my past through much introspection and reflection. However, no physician has ever asked me about those causes. Although it has been reported that the cause(s) of MS may include genetic, infectious, geographic, dietary, and/or hormonal factors, I have never seen psychological trauma on that list.

Regardless of cause, I recognize that the MS scars that continue to act up in my life serve as an important communication channel between me and my body. I experienced an exacerbation about a year ago that included paresthesias (basically, "pins and needles") in my feet, and the more stressed out I became, the higher the sensations spread up my legs, like mercury rising in a thermometer. Symptoms like that are a clear sign that I need to protect myself and attempt to relax and are tremendously valuable in my ongoing effort to recognize my limits before I do real damage.

Thus, I was not pleased at all when a stranger approached me at a conference recently and asked, with no introduction, "Do you want to be cured of your MS?" and implied that he had access to said cure. This was more annoying than the many well-meaning folks who approach me to ask me if I am aware of such-and-such a treatment (I probably am). Because my disease-like most diseases, I would guess–exists for a specific reason and serves a specific purpose, it is almost arrogant of me (and, certainly, of that guy) to attempt to erase it in one fell swoop without addressing the underlying causes. If I could wave a magic wand and cure my MS, I wouldn't do it because I don't know the potentially scarier ways my body might try to get its messages to me without that disease as a vector.

So I was very encouraged to discover that Debra and Sheri's healings often include metaphysical lessons. This component, as well as Debra and Sheri not being invested in a particular outcome and trusting that what happens is for the best, is what appeals to me about more formal energy healing practices like Johrei, in which the practitioner systematically aims the healing energy at you but doesn't take any credit or responsibility for what happens next. The result is between you and the energy.

I cannot stress enough that I am not suggesting here that everyone (or anyone) should adopt this philosophy regarding disease. For infection or injury (for example, broken bone, strep throat, or appendicitis), an allopathic physician would be my first stop. Foregoing standard treatment options can be a dangerous endeavor and should always be contemplated carefully. That being said, I believe that, just like allopathic medicine, healing methods often called "alternative" (though they are usually well-established and eons older than Western medicine) may be an important option for the myriad ailments a person may encounter during his/her life. In addition, scientific evidence for the modern usefulness and reliability of any treatment (ancient or contemporary) should be considered.

As a scientist, I am intrigued by the possibility of performing controlled, objective, empirical research documenting changes in healing status and verifiable information about the past and the future (themes 1, 2, and 3 listed above) and qualitative research examining the metaphysical components of disease (theme 4). The sharing of the cases reported here is an important first step on that journey and I look forward to the potential research opportunity.

Julie Beischel, PhD


Dr. Julie Beischel received her doctorate in Pharmacology and Toxicology with a minor in Microbiology and Immunology from the University of Arizona in 2003. She is the co-founder and Director of Research at the Windbridge Institute for Applied Research in Human Potential, a full member of the Society for Scientific Exploration and the Parapsychological

Association, and serves on the scientific advisory boards of the Rhine Research Center and the Forever Family Foundation. In addition to the metaphysical causes of disease, her research interests include the potential social applications of mediumship readings in bereavement and law enforcement. Dr. Beischel is Adjunct Faculty in the School of Psychology and Interdisciplinary Inquiry at Saybrook University and Director of both the Spirits and Spirit Communication and the Survival and Life After Death research departments at the World Institute for Scientific Exploration. She is the author of *Among Mediums: A Scientist's Quest for Answers.*

"Hope is powerful. It has the power to heal the mind and the body and the soul." Debra and Sheri

# CHAPTER ONE
## EVERYTHING WE LEARNED, WE LEARNED FROM GOD

The following is the true story of how Debra and Sheri became one with God.

It all started nineteen years ago when they met and became friends and also became ONE together on a spiritual journey. Then on August 31, 1997, Debra and Sheri were in a horrific accident when divine intervention came to save them both. They were passengers in a car traveling on a busy Phoenix highway when a van crossed two lanes to exit and hit their small sports car. Debra saw the van approaching a split second before impact. She immediately prayed aloud, *God, not now. We have children who need us. God, help us! God, help us!* The van ended up hitting their car and flipped over twice, landing on the other side of the guardrail. Sheri, seated in the front passenger seat prior to impact, was thrown into the crumpled backseat and ended up next to Debra in a tiny space. Debra and Sheri and the driver of the car were trapped and could not open the door.

A man appeared out of nowhere and managed to open the door and got all the women safely to the side of the freeway. He tended to Debra's injuries and then kissed her on the forehead and said, "I will see you again." The man turned to Sheri, kissed her, and gave her the same message. In the time it took Debra and Sheri to glance at the commotion caused by the first responders, the man disappeared. The severity of the accident necessitated five fire trucks, three ambulances, the fire chief, two tow trucks, and three or four police cars on the scene. Curiously, not one of these responders ever saw the man who saved the women.

Though both prayed and believed in God before the accident, the traumatic experience shifted something inside Debra and Sheri and opened their awareness to the other side. They firmly believed the mysterious man had been sent by God to save them. Their lives were changed completely and this is when their spiritual journey began. They were in a lot of pain physically–Sheri had injuries to her knee, back, and neck; Debra sustained severe neck and head trauma–but through this pain they were given the awareness that life is fragile and not to take one single moment for granted. The focus in their lives changed to growing spiritually, and they were inspired by a higher source: God.

In 2000, Debra was in another horrific automobile accident while on the way to Sheri's house. She was stopped at a stop sign when someone slammed into the back of her car. A man who was having a diabetic seizure hit her going approximately eighty miles per hour. Immediately upon impact, she crossed over to another dimension and witnessed everything that was happening to her here on Earth from above. She could hear herself thinking, *There is no way I am going to survive this crash!* She then felt a strong presence next to her and heard a voice ask, "Are you ready?" Debra was unmarried and had three children who needed her. As soon as Debra said the word "No," she found herself sitting in the backseat of her crushed car with a mouth full of glass. This accident opened the path to Debra's mediumship.

As a child, Debra could see spirits but they frightened her. Therefore, out of fear, she closed off this gift. After this car crash, she knew she was sent back for a reason. She had heard a voice, but whose voice did she hear? It took many years until she received an answer. This is what she heard in prayer: "There is only the one (meaning God) that can decide if you die or get a second chance." At this moment she knew that she had stood next to God and it was His voice that gave her a choice to live or die that day.

After this realization, she started doing readings for family, friends, and a small number of clients. In these readings she was able to share with them what she was hearing, seeing, feeling, smelling, and even sometimes craving from a loved one on the other side. One particular reading stands out. As she finished up the reading, a book called *The Afterlife Experiments* by Dr. Gary Schwartz fell off the shelf. Believing it was meant for her, she read Dr. Schwartz's book and was soon drawn to another title, *The Afterlife Codes* by Susy Smith. What happened next is amazing.

Debra felt the need to reach out to Dr. Gary Schwartz at the Human Energy Systems Laboratory (HESL) in Tucson, Arizona, which conducts research on the evolution of consciousness. She wanted to tell Dr. Schwartz that she received a message from author Susy Smith, who was deceased. Debra knew from the books she read that Dr. Schwartz and Susy had been good friends. She also wanted to be tested in his lab so that she could validate that what she was receiving from the afterlife was real.

Dr. Schwartz sent his colleague Dr. Julie Beischel to Debra's house to meet with her and discuss the VERITAS Research Program. The VERITAS Research Program of the HESL in the Department of Psychology at the University of Arizona was created primarily to test the hypothesis that consciousness (or personality or identity) of a person survives physical death. Dr. Schwartz was the director of the VERITAS Research Program and Dr. Julie Beischel was the co-director.

During their conversation, Debra told Dr. Beischel that she was in contact with the deceased Susy Smith and that Susy had a message to give to Dr. Schwartz. Dr. Beischel said, "Debra, I have something I need to share with you. Susy Smith was the founder of the Human Energy Lab. Before she passed, she said she would send mediums that we need to use in our lab and that they would come to us saying they have a message from her." Debra was shocked! Susy had been the one pushing her the entire time to get in contact with this lab. She was the one who made this all happen. Because of this, Debra dedicated her first book, *Believe Beyond Seeing*, to her.

From 1997 to 2012, Debra opened her door to the afterlife as a medium and her connection with God became stronger. She prayed for guidance not only for herself but also when she did her readings for others. She asked God for permission to connect to loved ones on the other side so that she could give her clients messages that comforted and healed those here as well as those she was connecting with.

Debra wasn't the only one whose connection with God was strengthening. In 2003, Sheri began having repetitive dreams that she was a healer and would be healing people individually and in groups all over the world. At the time, Sheri didn't believe she had the time to pursue a new career; her kids' activities kept her busy enough. One evening she found herself at a local bookstore when she was guided to a book about healing called *The Reconnection: Heal Others, Heal Yourself*. She devoured the book and immediately signed up to attend several seminars and trained to be a Reconnective healing practitioner. In 2004, she obtained the highest level of certification available and began doing healings on her family and friends.

It was January 21, 2012, when Debra crossed over and had a conversation with God. Debra had been sick for several months. She had not been able to eat, could barely drink, and it was hard for her to even walk from room to room. She was no longer able to drive or leave her house. She weighed only one hundred pounds and even speaking made her breathless.

The doctors at Mayo Clinic administered many tests and kept running into dead ends. They couldn't seem to find what was wrong. Debra became very frustrated. Why was this happening to her? Why was she so ill? Why couldn't they figure this out? If she tried to eat or drink anything, she would be in extreme pain. She was also losing control of her bowels. This was when she lost all her dignity. She no longer had any hope and her candle within was barely burning. She began preparing herself to die by disconnecting from all her loved ones. She told God in her daily prayers that she was ready to die and begged Him to please take her now!

It was the morning of January 21st when Sheri showed up unannounced at Debra's front door. Debra was bewildered. Sheri lived an hour away and would never come without calling. Sheri told her that she had heard a strong voice that morning, telling her that she needed to come to Debra's house immediately.

Debra thanks God every day that Sheri listened to and trusted those words. She felt that Sheri had come to comfort her. But when Sheri asked her if they could go into her bedroom and do a private prayer together, they had no idea what was about to take place would save Debra's life and change them both forever!

It took too much strength for Debra to sit. So Sheri laid out a blanket on her bedroom floor and had Debra lie on it. They began by lighting a candle, holding each other's hands, and praying to God. Sheri then asked Debra, "If we can heal others, then why can't we perform a healing on you right now?"

As Debra lay on the blanket, Sheri held her hand and told her to relax and receive the energy. Sheri asked God, Jesus, and the Holy Spirit to come forth to heal Debra. Immediately Debra heard that Sheri needed to keep her right hand over Debra's head to anchor her.

Debra's spirit was going to transcend to another level, and if she didn't anchor Debra, she wouldn't be able to come back. Sheri was a little frightened and told Debra, "You better not leave." Sheri knew that Debra felt like she was dying and felt that she might just give up.

Debra then saw a metal rod being placed inside her body. It went straight down the front of her body from her neck to her pelvis. At the same time, Sheri felt like small pebbles were being drawn magnetically to her hands, as if she were attracting all the toxins from Debra's body. She also felt lots of spirits in the room, for the room became very cold.

Next Debra heard God say, "They are going to cut you open, Debra." Debra saw spiritual surgeons enter the room. She saw in vivid detail the incision being made on the right side of her abdomen. Debra was able to explain to Sheri what she was seeing as her body was being worked on. She was told that she had two blockages on one side. One of the doctors stuck his hand in her abdomen and squeezed what she thought was her pancreas really hard. The pain was almost unbearable. She was in so much pain that Sheri asked Debra, "Do we need to stop now?" Debra told her they needed to keep going.

Sheri continued to place healing energy into Debra with her left hand while keeping her right hand over Debra's head. It was difficult to watch her friend experience so much pain, and at times it appeared that Debra had stopped breathing. Sheri had a very real fear that Debra would not come back because of the tremendous pain she felt.

As the doctors squeezed again, Debra felt a huge burst. She saw an explosion of green pus.

It reminded her of a pimple popping, but on a much bigger scale. The blockage in this area had now been cleared. At once Debra tasted metal in her mouth, and heard, "You have many metals in your body. We are now going to the next blockage." The doctors pushed from the top middle of her rib cage down past her belly button. This area was really blocked and was even more painful than the last blockage that had been cleared. Debra could feel the doctors pushing downward, and halfway through she felt the blockage, which they continued to push on to move it out. They did this at least ten excruciating times. Debra almost gave up this time for the pain was so intense. Finally, she felt it go through, almost like a ball going through a cylinder. The doctors had to push the ball out but once it was out, everything was clear.

Debra felt like she was taking her last breath. She felt her spirit effortlessly leave her body. Debra felt like she was floating; she was weightless. She saw a brilliant white light that got brighter as she went closer. Inside this white light stood a huge being, wearing a white robe that seemed to flow endlessly. As she got closer, she knew that this was God because He was grander and taller than any human. God's hands reached out for her. He picked her up and cradled her like a child.

Debra looked like a sick little child being held by her father. Her arms were down at her sides and her hair fanned over God's arms. She could not stand next to God this time; He had to carry her. All she could see was beautiful, pure white light, God's light shining all around her. God placed her body on a narrow table that looked like a balance beam. Once she was placed on the table, it turned into a beam of light. Next to this light was a beautiful glass coffin.

Debra wanted to sit in it because it was so beautiful. Since she was still able to speak to Sheri about what was happening, she described the coffin. Alarmed, Sheri shrieked, "Debra, do not get into that coffin!"

Debra noticed that although her body remained on the beam of light, her spirit, her soul, was now standing next to God. She took God's hands and He guided her to what looked like a cave. Inside the cave was a table. She took a seat at the table across from God.

God told Debra that she had been living on borrowed time since April 28th of the previous year. That was the day she heard His voice and as a result was protected from a deadly car accident. She had been driving on an Arizona interstate and had just missed her exit. Needing to get home, Debra decided to pull off on the shoulder of the road and back up slowly to take the exit ramp she had just passed. Just as she was about to drive onto the ramp, she heard a stern voice say, "Stop!" Surprised and shaken, she hit the brakes. She looked over her right shoulder just in time to see a semi-truck exiting the freeway at full speed. Had she not stopped exactly when she did, her car would have been obliterated by the truck. Debra realized that all the time since that instant had truly been a gift.

God said to Debra, "Your purpose on Earth has come to an end, but we come here today because I can alter your lifeline contract. You are all born with a lifeline contract. It holds all the details of your life and how and when you will die."

She was then presented with a choice: She could return to her broken body or stay with God, surrounded by an abundance of love. On the table in front of Debra was a contract. Written across the top was the word LIFELINE. Looking at the contract, she read these words:

> Health
> Joy
> Empowerment
> Prosperity
> Voice

After reading this, she still wasn't sure if she wanted to go back. The love here in heaven was so intense and she felt no pain; her suffering was over. She asked God if the chronic pain would be waiting for her if she returned to her body. As she stared at the contract, the word *Health* changed to *Healthy*.

God told Debra she would no longer have to deal with this illness. Still, she was feeling so much love that she was having a hard time deciding. She didn't have any thought of family or children or friends; she had already decided they would be okay if she died. Meanwhile Sheri worried about her friend. At times it appeared as though Debra had stopped breathing. More than once, Sheri told Debra in a stern voice, "I didn't come here to watch you leave! I came here to heal you through God!"

Ultimately it was Sheri who helped Debra make a decision. "Just sign the contract," Sheri insisted. Debra knew that Sheri had not suggested a healing session so that she could watch Debra pass over. Though Debra wanted to remain in heaven, she signed the contract to return to her body.

Sheri witnessed Debra's spirit re-enter her body. It moved like a wave from head to toe and then Debra took a breath as if for the first time. She heard Sheri say, "Are you coming back as the same person, the same Debra I know?"

After this healing, Debra's light within was again shining and she was full of hope. She had been given a new life. Though she needed time to recover from her spiritual surgery, within six months she was stronger and no longer had stomach pain.

Debra transitioned between life and death that day, and Sheri was with her every moment. This shared death experience left Debra and Sheri committed to fulfilling God's calling. (A shared death experience is a phenomenon where a near-death experience is actually shared by someone who is not dying, but who is emotionally connected to someone who is concurrently in the life-death transition.) Debra remembers God saying, "Always remember this date: 1-21-12. All numbers are reversible and so was your contract." God also told her that He had healed her but that she would never find out what was really wrong with her. If she did, then she would become attached to that word or illness. God was protecting her from knowing so that she would never let this be part of who she was or is today.

Debra still followed up with her doctors, but it was her choice to step in to the healing and to believe that God healed her. This took several months of hard work. She had to go deep within to see if she was holding on to anything from her past that needed to be released. With the help of God, she released a lot of things that she never realized she was holding on to.

Debra spent many hours in prayer and lighting her candle. During every step of her healing process, she trusted in God; she listened, she was guided, and she did what she was told, even when it was painful. She had to feel the pain in order to heal.

What Debra and Sheri do through God is limitless. Incredibly, as a result of signing her lifeline contract, Debra discovered that she had been given healing abilities. She was able to go to higher levels of consciousness while taking others on spiritual journeys, describing in specific detail what takes place during healing sessions. Sheri found that her healing abilities had also been enhanced after her role in Debra's healing. The energy in her hands was more intense, palpable. Her muscles ached from the sheer amount of energy that came through her body. She began to see peoples' auras, the different colors around their bodies. Sheri also felt the intensity of God's love for the people receiving healings. She sensed when God entered the room before Debra alerted her to His presence.

God gave Debra five words in her lifeline contract on that fateful day in January. Debra and Sheri now know the meaning of each of those words:

Healthy: Not only was Debra restored to full health, she and Sheri now have the ability to heal others.

Joy: The feeling Sheri and Debra experience every time they feel God work through them during their healing sessions. This joy feeds their souls.

Empowerment: God gave Sheri and Debra the strength to stand in His light and set His stage. They never waver and always trust in God.

Prosperity: Debra and Sheri now know that prosperity is not about the amount of money a person has in the bank.

True prosperity is about the connection with God and His presence in a person's life. Walking with and trusting in God is true prosperity.

Voice: God uses Debra's voice to send the messages He needs others to hear in order to be healed in their healing sessions. She gave Him her word that she would be His voice.

When Debra crossed over and spoke with God, Sheri asked her if she was coming back as the same Debra. Of course she wasn't. The old Debra died and the new Debra was born. A huge shift took place that day; it was the beginning of a new mission and duty for both of them.

Without Sheri's healing hands, Debra would not have had her experience. By saving Debra's life, Sheri signed up to do this healing work with God. They believe their healings carry a vibration that travels like electricity, instantly going directly into the person who is receiving the healing. God uses them as His instruments to see, hear, and feel what needs to be healed and to voice His words.

On January 21st—1-21-12—Debra signed a contract. She gave her word that she would become God's voice. On that day, God told her that all numbers are reversible and so was her lifeline contract. If she changed her mind about healing others, if she decided she could no longer be God's voice, she would return to heaven. Her purpose on Earth would be over.

Their journey has not been without hardship. They have experienced doubt, ended relationships, and yearned for the material comfort of their "old" lives. But Debra and Sheri feel they have gained so much more than has been lost. After all, God also signed the lifeline contract. God always honors His word, and He will never let Debra and Sheri down if they do His work.

Their lives are filled with God's love as they walk with their Heavenly Father every day. They trust that God is leading the way and they are devoted to serving Him on their mission. They have given the control to God, with whom all things are possible.

# CHAPTER TWO
# SPIRITUAL ADVENTURES
# AND MESSAGES

Sedona, Arizona, has long been considered a place of sacred beauty. Visitors travel to Sedona on quests of spiritual renewal. Debra and Sheri have made many such journeys to this enchanting town, and consider Sedona a place where they can remove themselves from their everyday lives and receive insight and information directly from God.

The trust they have in one another has been built from their shared love of God and the valuable information they receive. Their intent on these journeys is to obtain knowledge, insight, and balance, and they always walk away inspired.

The following pages contain words given to Debra and Sheri by God during many meditation and prayer sessions in Sedona. These messages planted the idea for them to write this book. Dates the messages were received are included to show how the theme of the book transpired in the years prior to their healing work. By opening their hearts and minds, they consciously allowed their Creator to express Himself through them. (Items in quotation marks are words received from God unless otherwise attributed.)

May 23, 2005
Debra and Sheri are shown a pyramid in meditation and told that it is the opening through which energy is sent, much like

the opening of heaven. Years later they would begin conducting their healing sessions under a pyramid in the Threshold Room at The Logos Center in Scottsdale, Arizona.

May 4, 2006
"Our mission together is to heal souls, one soul at a time. They will come to you by word of mouth. Your gift is a powerful one. You help people realize in a higher power. We will work through you to the sick and weary."

February 15, 2007
"You have come to teach others how to bridge the gap of human consciousness. You will continue to get visions, to journal, and share these visions with the masses. You will have a healing center in Arizona and the center will draw crowds from around the world."

October 4, 2009
"Stay still and listen, for it is the voice of God. You are about to raise your consciousness to a new heightened level of thinking. This can only be done when your body is clear of all toxins by purifying and drinking lots of water. Think clearly and purely. Only put food in your body that is pure and from the ground. Avoid all chemicals and processed food. Your body is a vessel and you must treat it as one in order to receive messages."

January 3, 2010
"There is power in the words that you are given. Never think it is you–you are a vessel that I am speaking through. Always know and trust this because this will give you the strength and fortitude needed to write this book."

May 1, 2010
"You will teach and heal those who cross your path."

July 11, 2010

"The words that you are given will be very detailed and must be written as such. Do not put your own words as these words are pure and come from me. These are not your thoughts as you are the channel and the message comes from me. Be very clear with this because many around you will not trust the words. There is no need to defend these words as you are the channel and the words come through you, not by you. Do not decipher them or second-guess. Just write them down and trust as you have prayed and know they come from the Highest Divine, from God. You are a vessel and may not be familiar with the information you are given. This is where you must trust in the Lord's words. This is a spiritual mission that you have agreed upon."

August 13, 2010

"They will not be long chapters, just very direct chapters. Each chapter has a specific direction to follow. Pay close attention to detail and do not leave any words out that have been given to you. You can add to the beginning and the end but the words have to stay in order."

August 17, 2010

"There is a shift occurring on this planet right now, a shift that is bringing about uncertainty and fear. This is a time where people need to stay grounded and certain truths revealed to them. These truths will set them free and start a path and journey to their own explorations.

"Be prepared for information that may sound a bit startling to you. As you know, these are not your own words as they are being written through you. Do not fear these words, as they are truths that have been hidden deep within our societies for hundreds and hundreds of years. It is now time for these truths to be spoken and written so people can make their own judgments. We have hidden power within each one of us. We no longer have to look for these outside sources to bring us this power. Within each of us are codes that can be activated and that hold truths about our potential as a person, codes that will start us on our own journey to exploration, where we do not have to look outside of ourselves. These codes empower us to be better people and to self-heal. These codes are so powerful that they will enable us to know exactly what to do to heal ourselves. Take great pride in this work as it is sacred and God's work."

August 25, 2010
"Speak your truth. Do not let anyone stand in the way of your truth. When you have prayed, when you have asked, and you have received, then you know and trust the truth. Believe in yourself and do not waver. Your journey is to spread the truth. You sit in devotion day after day and ask for truths. Now it is time to reveal these truths to yourself and others. Words will come to you in waves; write them down and they will be in your book. Trust in the words and trust in yourself.

May 10, 2010
"Your door is open and all you need to do is walk through to accept your gifts. Your job is to teach people how to go within and unlock the doors. Now is the time to find God within yourselves. It is internal, not external. You are teachers and your words are powerful and they will be heard by millions of people around the world in book form.

"You took an oath today with God. Are you willing to lose those you love? For this work will be too big for them to handle." Debra and Sheri replied, "We will always put you, Lord, first." God said, "I am the voice within you. You will voice my voice. You do the work and I will bring you the people."

October 26, 2010

"You are raising your level of consciousness daily through exercise and meditation. This is right where you should be; do not push, as this is a natural flow of energy moving through you. The words will come for your book at the right time. This will be effortless and you will not have to push for them. Everything is in perfect order and you must trust this."

March 11, 2011

At Cathedral Rock in Sedona, Debra and Sheri are told during meditation that they needed to connect to the pyramid.

July 11, 2011

"God has control, you don't. Stop trying to have control. This isn't about you, it is about God. So let go and trust. Trust is more powerful than control."

February 8, 2013

God gave Debra and Sheri the title of the book: *Direct Connect to God.* They had transcribed the entire book and placed it on the altar at The Logos Center when they heard the title.

August 30, 2013

God showed Debra a vision of a stage and was told by God that they would be setting the stage for Him.

"We as people have more power that lies within each of us. All one needs to do is access this by trusting that his own power is connected to our Heavenly Father, God."
Debra and Sheri

# CHAPTER THREE
# INTUITIVE ENERGY HEALERS –
# HOPE, HEALING & MIRACLES

In defining themselves as intuitive healers, Debra and Sheri draw a distinction about their work. Their intuition extends to a direct connection with God. Intuitively, Debra and Sheri do not know the person receiving the healing, nor do they know what this person needs. Only God knows what is needed.

Sheri and Debra want to share the knowledge they have learned through their nineteen-year spiritual journey together. Through their life trials, spiritual guidance, and God, they were given a higher awareness of consciousness, including a profound new technique that they have developed and made their own for their healing sessions. Debra and Sheri set their humanness aside and allow God to use them as His instruments.

God uses Sheri's hands as His instruments during each session. Sheri places healing energy into the body with her palms. She feels the higher and lower frequencies as her hands hover over the body and uses those frequencies as a guide. She also removes what is no longer needed and does not serve the body.

Debra still uses her abilities as a medium to see, hear, and feel from Spirit, but now she is also able to see, hear, feel, and voice messages from God. She can actually see and hear what is taking place inside and outside the body during the healing session and is told by God what needs to be healed. During these healings, Debra becomes one with each person who is receiving a healing. By becoming one with the person, Debra is able to know what the person is feeling and thinking during the healing. At the same time, God speaks through Debra, His words directed to each individual.

God will have Debra physically feel what needs to be healed, which guides her to the areas that need to be treated. God has Debra feel this pain so that there is no denying the areas that need to be healed. Through this pain it becomes real. This pain is intense and can be physical or emotional. She knows when a spiritual surgery is taking place because not only does she see the spiritual surgeons, she also tastes the medicine being administered. Sheri sees with her naked eye the physical transformation that takes place in Debra's body during healing sessions. Together, through God, they are able to get to the root of what is causing the unbalance in the body and then release it. The recipient of the healing is then told what caused his or her sickness or unbalance.

God will send His spiritual surgeons from the other side to perform these spiritual surgeries, using Debra and Sheri as His instruments. Debra and Sheri share a strong trust in one another and in God, which allows them to do these healings and to stand strong behind what they hear, feel, and express to the people they heal. They stand strong in the words they hear from God and they never waver. If they did not have this trust, they would not be able to deliver the messages that come through.

No two healings are the same. Each person is given what he needs in that moment. Debra and Sheri do not know what is happening in each person's life. They do not know each individual's situation. They are not told anything about the person receiving the healing except for a name. Debra and Sheri open up their hearts, minds, and souls to give each person what is needed in that moment. It could be strength, courage, balance, knowledge, or just the ability to feel the presence of God in that moment. When they as healers step into the room, they surrender all outcomes to God, as it is not up to them. God is in control and knows what each individual needs at that moment. They trust and know that a higher power is at work.

They as healers always want the miracle, but if they are walking in God's light, then they have to trust the outcome. They have to trust that each person who steps before them is receiving exactly what he needs at that moment. It is not up to Sheri and Debra as they are only a piece of the puzzle. As they step in to do their part of the healing, it is up to each individual to also do his part.

As healers, their part is to be God's instruments and give God's love through themselves, which would be Sheri's hands and Debra's voice. They are only part of the process and the rest is up to God and the person receiving the healing. It is up to Him whether a healing comes instantaneously or if it is a longer process

By just stepping into the healing room, one is in the presence of God, and that alone has immense healing powers. These transformational healings are the key to bringing balance, peace, joy, and love into your life. It is recommended that a person come in to the session with no expectations, for what one thinks is needed may not always be what is received. It is up to each person to be responsible and to do his part in the healing process and to trust God fully, to thank God for the healing that has just begun.

## What happens during a healing session

Before a session begins, three candles are lit by Sheri, Debra, and the person receiving the healing. This represents that they are all becoming one with God, meaning that Debra and Sheri give God permission to use them as His instruments and vessels. They open all of their senses in order to see, hear, feel, taste, and smell what happens in the healing room. Debra and Sheri's intention during healing sessions is to witness miracles. The miracles do not come from them but from God.

When the presence of God enters, He comes in a form that each woman recognizes. Debra's vision of God, for instance, is larger than life. When standing next to Him, she feels so small, like a child looking up to her father. She sees a white robe that drapes down. God has the bluest eyes, a blue that has never been seen here on Earth. God made His son Jesus to look just like Him.

There is a definite shift of energy in the healing room when God enters. This also happen in larger venues too. People feel the presence of God and hear His words come through Debra. An undeniable love settles on those at the healing session, embracing them on the inside and often making them cry on the outside.

During a healing session, they may feel the temperature change in the room. This is when Debra knows that loved ones from the other side are present. She may also taste medicine or see gloves being put on spiritual surgeons' hands to let her know God is going to have a spiritual surgery take place.

Taking people on spiritual journeys is a gift that God has given Debra. She is able to take them to many levels that no one has been before. Most of the time, people will visualize in their minds what Debra is explaining and seeing during a journey. While their physical bodies are anchored and monitored by Sheri in the room, their spirits are lifted and go on a spiritual journey to many different levels. Debra never knows at which level they will arrive, nor does she know what is going to take place. She allows God to guide her. This could not happen without the trust she has with Sheri, knowing she can effortlessly leave and return with her assistance.

## The Threshold Room

Some of the healings in this book were performed at The Logos Center in the Threshold Room in Scottsdale, Arizona.

The Threshold Room is a ten-by-ten-foot dedicated meditation room. The entire room is enclosed in a Faraday cage which shields the walls, floor, and ceiling with copper screening and grounded copper rods. The metal door is also grounded. This design approximates a completely shielded environment. Research has demonstrated that ESP accuracy is enhanced when the subject is shielded is this manner.

The room is equipped with a ten-foot square copper pyramid that has the angular proportions identical to those of the Great Pyramid of Egypt. Associated with the pyramid is an amethyst grid complete with large amethyst stones at each corner and the apex of the pyramid.

## Words said at the beginning of each healing session

In the following chapters, these words have been removed from the text of each healing. Please know these words were said and are said before each and every healing that Debra and Sheri perform. The words are recited as the person receiving the healing lies on the healing table. Debra stands at the foot of the table, holding the person's ankles, while Sheri stands at the top of the table and holds the person's shoulders.

"I want you to imagine a beam of white light and that beam of white light goes up to our heavenly Father, God. God holds on to that white light. And that white light comes all the way back down and enters your belly button. God holds this white light. It goes all the way up to heaven and back. And when it does that, it secures you to the table like a seat belt, holding you in God's love, light, and healing. I, Debra, remove my humanness and I will allow God to use me as His vessel and as His instrument so that I can see what needs to be healed, feel what needs to be healed, and hear the words that you need to hear for this healing.

"When I feel pain, do not worry. This is a gift from God. For when I feel this pain, it makes what is taking place undeniable. I have to feel it to know it and then to deliver it. I will not take on this pain; when I leave this room, it all goes away. I am just feeling the pain during the healing and then it is released once I leave this room.

"When I voice these words to you, know that they are not my words, these are God's words. He uses my voice as His to deliver the messages you need to hear, for I do not know you but God knows you and knows what it is you need to hear. If I take you on a spiritual journey, I will guide you. You may feel weightless or you may not feel anything at all. I will describe what is taking place. Sometimes people will feel like they are on the journey with me and sometimes people will visualize in their minds what is taking place. If a spiritual surgery takes place, God will send spiritual surgeons into the room. You may hear me say I taste medicine, as this is a sign a surgery is going to take place. If I say the word 'they,' this word refers to spiritual surgeons. God will oversee the entire healing.

"I may also see loved ones from the other side come into the room. Sometimes I will know who they are and sometimes I will just say a loved one is here, watching over and loving you during this healing.

"When Sheri enters the room, she removes her human-ness and she allows God to use her as His instrument. And God will speak to her in her mind, guiding her to where she needs to be on the body. She will feel the higher and lower frequencies on the body, placing healing in and taking out what is not serving the body. What's most important is that God uses her hands as His hands to place the healing energy into your body. Sheri holds the energy in the room. She will also monitor us and anchor us if we take a spiritual journey together. This allows us to leave and come back effortlessly.

"What you need to know is that when you lie on this table, your entire body is being scanned, touched, and healed from your head to your toes. I, Debra, then go underneath the table and lie parallel to you in order to become one with you. When I become one with you, that is when I will start to receive."

"I am the way, I am the truth, and I am the light. Those who stand in it become one with me. And those who become one with me become the way, become the truth, and become my light." - Debra and Sheri

# CHAPTER FOUR
# FURTHER PROOF OF HEAVEN

## Dr. Eben Alexander Healing Session
## November 11, 2012

D r. Eben Alexander, a renowned academic neurosurgeon and author of the *New York Times* best-selling book *Proof of Heaven*, spent over three decades honing his scientific worldview. He thought he knew how the brain, mind, and consciousness worked. A transcendental near-death experience (NDE) in which he spent a week deep in a coma from an inexplicable brain infection changed all of that completely!

Debra and Eben had a strong connection from the first time they met. They shared the common bond of having their lives changed by near-death experiences. In one of their early conversations, Debra invited Eben to The Logos Center to experience his own healing session. He accepted, and upon arriving at the healing center, Eben, Debra, and Sheri were soon talking like old friends.

The mood changed when they entered The Logos Center. Everyone became very serious. Eben stepped into the Threshold Room on his own, where he knelt and prayed by the healing table. At the same time, Debra and Sheri held hands at the altar of the church and prayed for Eben's healing. They felt that God had orchestrated this gathering and also that something miraculous was going to take place. This all set the tone for Eben to be open and ready for his healing session to begin.

The Healing Session

Sheri asks Eben to lie on his back on the healing table. She stands at the top of the table by his head and Debra is at the other end of the table by his feet. Sheri touches his shoulders as Debra touches his ankles and the three become one with God.

Debra begins, "The first thing we do is ground you to the table with the white light that comes through the center of a pyramid. It goes all the way up to heaven where God holds it. That beam of light comes down and goes through your solar plexus/ belly button and it grounds you from here to there and there to here so that you are in pure love. It is this light from God that grounds you to the table, but also allows you to leave. So if you want your spirit to leave and to travel somewhere and go to a different dimension, you can do this because you know your body is safe, that you are held by God and will be able to return with ease. We surround this room with pure white light and everything that comes through here is from God."

Debra explains that because of this white light beaming down, Eben will not be able to move the center of his body. "You will no longer be able to move your mid-section as you are locked to the table so that you know that you are safe. What I do is I lie down parallel to you on the floor underneath the healing table."

Eben answers, "Okay."

At this time, Sheri further connects with Eben. She starts by sending energy to Eben's mind through his temples. This aligns Eben with an energy frequency and vibration. It also relaxes him. Eben's eyes are closed but Sheri can tell that he is connected to this energy flow by the way his eyes move back and forth under the eyelids.

"Then here we go," Debra says. "Take in three deep breaths. I'm going to be lying next to you on the floor as there is work to be done. I'm seeing to the right of you a doctor and he's putting his gloves on. Snap, snap–the gloves are now on." She explains that spiritual surgery could be painful for him but that she will be intercepting much of that pain as it slowly gets released.

"What happens, Eben, is it's all in your heart chakra. And I see a sword going deep, deep, deep." Debra describes how the doctors are going to pull the sword out. With this extraction will come a healing of his heart. She says that someone placed that sword in him. "It hurt you. It hurt you bad. It is like being stabbed in the heart. So we are going to pull this out right now. You are going to feel it. Don't resist. Just allow it." She says the doctors are pulling hard but he's still resisting. "Don't resist it. Believe you deserve this! Now in your mind, release it!"

Debra expresses that the first sword has been pulled out. "There was so much hurt there, it was like having a huge hole in your heart. We do not want your heart to bleed, so we are going to have the doctors fill it, seal it, and replace it with the love of God. They are going to suture it. That is why the surgeon is here. He is mending your hurt." Sheri works intensely, pulling this weight off of Eben. The energy force is strong and takes a lot of physical energy to remove. As Sheri takes this energy out, she passes it on to God.

Debra reassures Eben that he is loved, then continues describing how his pain runs so deep from even before he was born. "You felt unwanted. So they are taking that seed out of you and they are mending it. You didn't have a cord that was attached. You never felt attached. You never had the love of attachment. This is all being healed right now." Debra continues, "God is putting in a new attachment and the attachment is now to God. It is a pure cord, a cord of love and a cord of truth." She describes how this new cord will allow Eben to lessen his feelings of needing to protect himself and to let down his shield. Debra tells him, "Release that wall. I know this is painful. Just let it go, let it go. Let God have it, give it to

Him. Because this isn't something you caused. This isn't what you wanted. This was put in you. You don't need to feel this anymore; give it back to God. Let Him give you the purity of what you were supposed to have been born with." Now Debra talks about going to another level. "You felt there was no love and who did you turn to? You didn't even have God's love at that time. But guess what? Now you do! Your abandonment is now replaced with God's love and His connection and His cord. This cord will always remain in you. It is now connected to you. It will never, ever go away. You can feel it here now, always."

Debra continues, "This all has to do with your heart. So what has happened is you have built thorns around your heart and these thorns became thicker and thicker. So what we are going to do is we are going to cut these thorns and we are going to take them away from your heart because they are preventing you from receiving the love you deserve. So now we are going to cut these thorns. You are going to feel them snapping and you might even hear them snap. It's like the doctors are in there and they are cutting the thorns and they are unwrapping them from your heart right now. They are being pulled and unraveled. There are many, many, many layers for them to take out. And I know it's painful, and I am so sorry, but we are just taking these layers off.

"Okay, now I am going to tell you something else. I am hearing that there is a lot you have done in your past that has put negative energy on your heart. That's just because you didn't know. You used this energy, thinking you could hide from it. You thought it was making you feel better but really it wasn't. It took you to a dark space. We have to take it off of the heart, so Sheri is going to place healing energy from God on your heart. It's coming off and it is from the past so you no longer want to carry it with you. Sheri is pulling out, pulling out the negative strands because you no longer have to carry them. Use everything you have to get this out, Eben. Sheri is pulling…pull, pull, you can do it! It is going to come out! There it goes, it is gone. It is gone!" Debra pauses, collecting her strength.

Removing this deeply rooted cord of pain takes all of Sheri's energy and strength, and it takes Debra speaking the words of God and Eben's effort to release. Debra says, "This was very painful. Your heart is filled with divine, heavenly, pure love; nothing else will ever come in. We are going to seal your heart so that it is now protected. It is shielded and protected and nothing will harm you. Nothing will hurt you and you will not go to the darkness to find pure love because the love is here and will never, ever leave you."

Debra continues channeling: "This is a gift from God. It does another thing for you too, and that is it now makes your heart also your eyes. That is what I am being told. Your heart becomes your eyes so that when you use your eyes and when you look into the souls of other people, you will know if they are there for you with pure love or if you need to turn around and not trust them. So instead of you putting up a block because you didn't have the trust, now you have a trust within you that is called God's trust. He is going to allow you to see it through your heart. And it will instantly click in your subconscious, yes or no. You will know! And you will feel it in your gut. That is the gift you just received."

Sheri adds, "There's so much energy going through my hands into you, Eben. If you look at my hands, every place they are moving to is just pure love going directly to you from God."

Debra continues, "The gift that you are getting is the gift of trust. And that is what God is telling you right now, to trust. So at this time I want you, Sheri, to shield Eben with God's light and seal this healing before we take the next journey."

Sheri takes over. "So what we are going to do is place the seven seals of God's white light and love down the body and seven seals up the body. This bonds the healing that just took place. It will never leave you, Eben. You have access to this energy at any time." When Sheri seals, she motions with both hands, creating seven triangles down the body and seven triangles up the body.

Debra announces that this particular healing has now been sealed and asks if Eben would like to go on a spiritual journey. He answers yes. She continues to explain that they will be going out of their bodies.

Debra begins by guiding the spirit out through the top of her forehead. Sheri stands near the head, grounding and sending energy while this is happening. Debra says, "Eben, you are just going to take a deep breath in and push out. Push out again. I am standing by the side of the table; come join me. One more push. And now we are holding hands. So you see me and we are now standing next to each other. I just looked at you and I smiled. Take my hand, and we are going to take this journey. Oh my gosh, that blue butterfly just showed up. Oh my gosh, this has never happened before!"

Debra is overwhelmed with emotions. Seeing this butterfly gives her insight into what is about to take place. She knows that the blue butterfly is significant in two ways: One, a blue butterfly appears on the cover of Eben's book. Two, Eben once told her that he had ridden a blue butterfly during his near-death experience. Debra is sure that they are going to take a ride. She asks, "Where do I sit, Eben? You lead me."

Eben says, "Right here, right in front of me."

"Here we go, Eben, here we go, oh my gosh, here we go!" Both are laughing. Debra is very giddy, like a little girl at an amusement park. This was really taking place on a different dimension that one does not get to experience here on Earth. Sheri continues her energy work and hears the joy in their voices as Debra expresses her delight.

"Oh my gosh, we are there, we are there, Eben! It's flying so fast. I feel like I have to hang on because we're swerving and diving. We're now going to land in the pasture. We're coming down and we're going to get off the butterfly. Okay, we're off the butterfly and we're standing in this meadow, but the grass is long. Our feet are in this long, flowing grass." It's not like the grass on Earth. The grass they see is very animated and vibrant. Each blade is long, pointed at the top, and lush, dark green. The blades wave back and forth as if the wind were moving each one. The pasture seems endless, though there is a path in front of them.

"Do you see the path, Eben, it's curved?" He nods. "We're going to walk down this path. The butterfly is going to stay here. So here we go. We're walking down a white path. Do you see the white light ahead? Here we go!"

The energy in the room shifts. All three feel the presence and love of God. It is so intense it brings them all to tears.

Debra grabs Sheri's ankle from her place below the healing table with her right hand and holds Eben's left hand. Sheri holds Eben's right hand as she leans over him. All three are being infused. All three are becoming one as a white light engulfs them.

Sheri instinctively asks, "Are you ready to go back?"

"Yes," Eben replies.

Now God speaks through Debra again. "Eben, you have more work than you thought you had here. And the work is amongst us. The work has to be done together as we are one. And we joined hands and we became one. It can only be done as one." Debra then says she feels so light-headed that she might faint. "I feel weightless. Weightless like I am totally floating, floating to many levels. My body is shaking. Eben, God is looking at us. He is looking straight at us, eye to eye, soul to soul. You can feel it and see it because we are one. But there is a message:

"Go walk in my feet and do my work and speak my truth. The light has now been put within. You have been infused as one. The power is within you; three is more than one. So when you do it together, the power will be even more. You need to use each other as grounding tools because if you use each other, you balance. You work as a team and that team is me. I guide the team. I lead the way, but you need to trust it. Put on my shoes, these are my feet, I am your voice, this is the truth. You are going to turn around now and do my work. My work is done within you, but your work is not done. It has just begun. And it will be bigger than anything you have ever known. It is limitless, and it is weightless, like it is here. Allow yourself to soar because that is what you are doing. You are soaring, you are flying."

A pole of light is going through Debra, Sheri, and Eben, right through the guts. It is very painful and all three are feeling the intensity. Extreme light of God is going all the way up and all the way down through the table and through them.

Debra says, "The light is coming in. Pure white light and love and what happens is when we are done, people will see this light shining outward. People will see the light through our eyes. We will pierce them. They will have a hard time even looking at us. This is all it is. It is God's white light coming through us. It's done! We are done!"

Debra sees a loved one arrive from the other side. "Eben, your sister is smiling and says, 'I told you this, I told you this, I told you this.' She stands in white with her hand out. She floats up and down. You can feel her presence. You get to see her again. Turn to your right and you will see her standing. She is there, look at her. She wants you to go back and eat cookies for her!"

Debra starts singing, "We are one in the spirit, we are one in the Lord, we are called to do our work now, we will serve, do your service, we will do your service." She had heard the angels singing these words. The beautiful tone was a pitch that isn't heard in human form.

Sheri prepares them for the journey back by invoking the following: "This healing will never leave us." She motions with her hands to convey the seven seals of God's white light to

bond this journey and healing. The energy runs so power-
fully through Sheri that she can't take her hands off of Eben's
head. Sheri looks under the table to check on Debra, who is
crying uncontrollably. Debra looks up and shakes her head.
Sheri knows Debra does not want to come back. Sheri says in
a stern voice, "Eben, you need to bring her back now. Get her
on that butterfly." It takes Sheri several times to get his attention. Then Sheri says, "Debra, you are coming back!" Debra
and Eben get back on the butterfly. The spiritual journey is
now complete.

❧ ❧ ❧

Dr. Eben Alexander's relationship with Debra and Sheri has
grown into a true friendship. He is like family to them.

God can do what medicine cannot do.

A **miracle** is a surprising and welcome event that is not explicable by natural or scientific laws and is therefore considered to be the work of a divine agency.

# Chapter Five
# A True Miracle from God

**Dr. James Veney Healing Session**
**January 17, 2014**

In the Words of Dr. James Veney
I am a retired professor of public health in the department of health administration at the University of North Carolina at Chapel Hill. I also worked for many years in developing countries with the World Health Organization and with USAID. What follows is my account of my healing with Debra and Sheri.

I think of 2013 as the lost year. In February I noticed that my energy level was declining. It turned out I had non-Hodgkin's lymphoma, and in April I began a treatment regimen of chemotherapy that laid me low. Most days I could hardly move from my chair. Any kind of physical activity was impossible, and I even gave up painting, one of my passions. Chemotherapy causes collateral damage, and in my case it was peripheral neuropathy that included tingling in my hands and numbness in my feet. Watching me struggle with my symptoms, my daughter arranged a healing for me with Debra Martin and Sheri Getten.

I am typically skeptical of anything that doesn't have a proven scientific basis, having spent my entire career doing research on effectiveness in the health field. But I knew it was important to both my daughters and my wife that I do this.

My family and I met with Debra and Sheri on Friday morning. I had no idea what to expect, and even now don't know exactly what happened. What I do know is that I lay on my back on a table in a darkened room at The Logos Center. Debra seemed to take on my thoughts and feelings and was able to sense my affliction, while Sheri assisted with the energy work, waving her hands over me. During the session, Debra talked about my pain; it seemed that she really could feel it. At the end of the session, my wife and daughters came into the room and we all said the Lord's Prayer. Truthfully, I didn't really feel any different than when I went in.

Three days later I went to my appointment with a lymphoma specialist at Banner MD Anderson Cancer Center in Gilbert, Arizona. Based on previous tests, he had already concluded that I had lymphoma in my central nervous system and proceeded to outline two treatment options. One included surgery to remove the cancer in my brain, chemotherapy injected into my spine, and radiation treatment, and the other would be just a regimen of chemotherapy for my spine. Neither treatment choice appealed to me, and the doctor said that the prognosis for me to be cured with even the most intensive regimen of treatment was only two to ten percent. He also indicated the need for another spinal tap to pinpoint the type of lymphoma that needed to be treated. As we left the clinic, my daughter assured him that there would be no need for treatment because there would be no lymphoma cells in the fluid drawn from my spinal column.

We returned to the cancer center two days later for the spinal tap and chemotherapy injection. Based on the gloomy predictions from the neurologist and oncologist, my wife and I were bracing ourselves for the worst. The oncologist had said he would call with the test results at the end of the week. The outcome: There was no evidence of lymphoma in my spinal fluid. MD Anderson is renowned for cancer diagnosis and treatment, so I am confident in the result of that test. I do not have cancer in my spinal column or in my brain. What I know is that I went to the healing and my symptoms disappeared. The cancer was completely gone within one week of my healing session. That is enough for me to be truly grateful for the help Debra and Sheri gave me. I feel I have a second chance!

The Healing Session
Debra and Sheri place their hands on Jim before the session begins. Debra touches his ankles and Sheri touches his shoulders. Debra says, "We are stepping in and becoming one and asking God what needs to be healed here and now." Debra kneels underneath the table and feels herself becoming one with Jim. Sheri starts to give him energy near both of his temples. As soon as Debra lies down and connects with Jim, she feels heaviness in her chest and lungs. She coughs and has a hard time breathing. It then starts opening up and it is a little easier to breathe.

Debra says, "It is so heavy that it feels like I am holding something on my chest, or you are holding something and it is causing you not to breathe. So it is taking some life out of you. This is something that you need to release to God, whether it happens in this room or whether you do it later. I just feel like there is something heavy, like a brick on your chest. And now that has left me."

For some reason, Debra can't move the center of her body, so she holds herself rigidly from her waist all the way up to her neck. She says, "They are aligning my head and even if I move it a little bit, I have to remain totally straight, like I am on a board. So I want you to know that everything is stiff, hard." Debra feels like she is bracing herself. She sniffs and says that she just received a bunch of medicine. She says, "When I receive medicine, I can taste it." She begins coughing. "There is pressure in the right side of my head. I also feel like my head is being locked down so if you were to have to work on these areas in a surgery, your head would be locked straight. It is almost as if there is a metal brace that would go around your head that would keep your head straight. Everything below is totally straight. So everything right now has to be aligned."

Debra has a hard time talking right now because everything has to be straight on her body. She says, "This is weird because it is affecting my mouth."

She then feels pain in her right shoulder blade and her back. The pain right now is excruciating and radiates right through the center of her back shoulder area. Her head remains incredibly straight. Debra has to put her hands on the legs of the healing table because she feels like she has so much pressure on her back that it hurts. The spiritual doctors are doing something that causes her a lot of pain. She puts her hands over her head and interlocks her thumbs because she was told this will help the pain she feels. She says, "This also is hurting my shoulders when I do this. They are pulling and I now feel totally straight."

She sees a white tube. She says to Jim, "I want you to imagine a vacuum that is white, like a cylinder, but it is bendable, though when it goes in it stays straight. It is like I am seeing hard plastic yet on the outside it is bendable, but when it goes on the inside it's stiff, so I don't know how this works but that is what I am being shown. I want you to imagine your spine and then I want you to imagine everything in between like your veins and your muscles. I want you to imagine that this tube can actually go over the bones and as it does it suctions everything out of the crevasses that you do not need in your body. The reason why it is plastic and hardened is so that they can capture what is being suctioned out."

Debra then cries out in pain and says she is getting a massive headache when they touch these areas. She receives more medicine which is directed to her head. She sees a surgeon working on her head by the right temple and over the forehead above the right eye. She says, "That is where I see him, but as they were suctioning down below, it went right to my head. There is so much heat I am feeling in my head right now, so much heat." She can barely stand the pain from the heat in her head. As she feels all of this heat in her forehead, Sheri asks Debra if she should continue working on Jim's head since Debra is in so much pain.

Debra says, "Oh my gosh, I can feel it radiating and burning so much. Imagine a tool that was thin like a pencil, but on the end was this light that was able to burn. I can't move my whole body and I have to keep my back straight and my head straight. I am so dizzy and feel like I have to throw up and just want to turn my head, but I can't. That pole is suctioning all the toxins out. They are working down below and now up above they are working on my eyes."

She is in so much pain as they work on both of her eyes that she has to grab Sheri's ankles to ground her and give her energy as Sheri gives Jim energy. She breathes very deeply and says, "Just know that they are working on the head and I just feel all this heat and radiation." She takes deep breaths and continues to hold Sheri's ankles.

Debra says, "When they work on it—the center of my back—I don't even know how to explain it. The center of my back feels sore, like inside. But it also touches my organs so it just feels achy right there." She breathes deeply. "Oh my gosh. I don't know which pain is worse because I feel both at the same time and it is hard to describe both pains at once."

She wants to cry because it hurts so badly and she can't leave this position because she is told that she has to stay still. She asks God to lessen the pain so she can stay in this position. She cries, "It hurts so bad on my spine. Lots and lots and lots of pain! Imagine as if you had a cut or somebody had to sew you up, like you needed stitches, but they didn't numb you. So you felt it all as they were doing the procedure. That is what I am feeling. I am feeling the pain while they are doing the procedure. I have to stay like this until everything is complete. This pain penetrates straight across, kind of where your upper back is; that is where I feel it right now."

She cries out in pain and says the spiritual surgeons are slowly working towards her shoulder now. Debra can feel the suctioning tube going straight through the center of her spine. She says her legs are numb and she wants so badly to stretch out and she can't.

Debra says she feels like everything is sore. All of her muscles ache, but she is now able to relax her arms. Her head still has to stay stiffly straight. Debra says, "I feel like there is a mother figure here on the right. I am not sure if you lost your mom, but it is on the right so it would be from your dad's side of the family... They corrected me. There is a mother figure standing on the right that is from your father's side. It is very cold in the room. When it is cold in the room, it means that there are many loved ones that are here for you. When I said that, it got even colder. That is one way for me to know that your loved ones from the other side are here."

Debra then says that she hears words coming in for Jim from God. "You know how to fight the fight. In your mind or in your soul you have thought, 'I don't know if I am as strong as I once was to fight.' And that is what you question. Before, you were younger and you were stronger and you just had that will. You had that unstoppable attitude and that's how you were able to move through life and become who you are. Nothing stopped you, you believed in it all. It doesn't matter what age you are for you to have the strength. So remove that way of thinking and know that I am within you. That same strength that was once there before is here again to help you walk forward and receive all of it you deserve. And you say, 'I was so blessed to have been given this time. I am just grateful that I was given this extended time.'"

Debra says, "I am being told to tell you that there are no limitations. There are no limitations on time. So don't look at it like, 'I was given the gift of time so I am blessed with what I had and I will take what I have been given.' Think instead, 'I walk forward knowing that my time is limitless and I still have the strength that I once had before.'"

Debra continues, "And with that way of thinking, it changes it all. I have been given more medicine so I know that the spiritual surgeons are now working in the head area again. They are going through the center of the head, not the forehead but the top of the head. She says to Sheri, "I want you to push white light through there." Then to Jim, "And James, I want you to imagine as Sheri pushes the white light in, that the white light is God's white light and He is going to surround all this area that needs to be healed here and now. I am getting an immense headache in my forehead as Sheri pushes the white light in."

Debra now smells a different type of medicine than normal. Debra wonders aloud if they administer different types of medicines for different procedures because she has never tasted this before. She says, "So as we envision this white light coming in–" She cries out in pain and asks Sheri to hold her head. Sheri never touches Debra during a healing session, so she had to lean down. "It feels like my head is going to explode!"

Debra says to Jim, "I want you to envision that this white light is going in and touching everything inside your brain, holding it, touching it, and seeping in where it needs to go. And as the white light touches all, it places the light and the love and the healing at the areas that need to be touched and healed."

Debra turns her head to the left and cries out in pain. She says, "They want to get into the side, that back part." Debra can feel her head and says, "It's almost as if I have electric vibes going through and I feel them as heat going up and in. It is going in and feeding those areas, the electricity.

"James, I feel that God just stepped into this room, right here and now, at this moment. He is standing at the end of the table by your feet. I want you to keep your eyes closed. I want you to envision that your body is lying here on the table, but God takes your hands and your spirit sits up. So your spirit is sitting up on the table, but your body is lying on the table. And as you sit up, you reach your hands out and you are able to hold God's hands at the end of the table. So you're holding His hands and He is holding your hands. And as you sit up, He is looking at you and you are looking at Him. And it is kind of weird because you can feel that your body is lying down but at the same time you can feel like you are sitting up. How can that be? Because I am giving you the vision of your spirit which is sitting up and holding hands. I feel a great presence of God and it is so intense that it makes me want to cry."

Debra's voice shakes as she feels the overwhelming presence of God standing in the room. She is not able to speak for a few moments because she is in awe. She then says, "He is saying to you that you did so well on your journey and you served your purpose to the fullest in everything that you were told to do; you came here and you did it. Like I said, you were unstoppable. You never want to look at yourself like, 'Wow, I am this gentle and kind man.' You don't have to look at yourself, for you can look through your daughters because it is a spitting image, a mirror image of you. You are one and the same. That is what I am honoring you for, the person that you are. The person you became and what you gave in this world. But as you sit here and I hold your hands, I just want you to know that you are not fighting this alone."

Debra's voice changes and she becomes very quiet and is nearly overcome with emotion as she speaks words from God. "And I know you feel so much pressure because everyone wants you here, and I am here to take that pressure off of you, to tell you that this is between you and me now. And we will walk this walk, but I want you to let your control go. Not your fight, not the will, but the control. And when I say control, it means that you are allowing me to take the control of your life, knowing what next is coming. And when you let that control go, it is freeing.

"And it will release all the pressure that you put on yourself. Everybody does not mean to give you those pressures. It is pure love, but you hold on to that and it is hard. So as I hold your hand, I am telling you, I am here to free you of that pressure, knowing that I am the one in control, not you. And if you walk that way, you know that I put you on this table, I know what you need the most, and when you walk forward, you will know this is my will. And you will go through all the proper steps and do everything you possibly know, but you know that either way you do not lose because God is the one doing it. Let that worry of how it is going to affect your family go, for I hold on to each one of them too. Trust in me. I am not going to leave."

Debra takes a deep breath and says, "During that time you were being spoken to, you were also being worked on and I felt like they were working on the inside of your head. I don't taste any medicine right now. I also feel a lot of heat radiating in my lower back, so you might feel pressure there. I do feel like they want you to rest because you know that anybody who goes through a real physical surgery, his body needs healing. The body needs to rest. The body needs proper care. So when you go home, you need to take this time to allow the healing to work and sleep and rest. Drink lots of fluids. Now I want to make sure that everything is realigned."

Debra tries to stretch out but it is very painful. "Your dad's side of the family was here very, very strong. I do feel like I got a little more medicine just now, so that means that they are numbing you in the different areas. It is like going home on medicine so you will be very tired. I feel like I want someone to step on my back because it hurts. They put a lot of fluids in you, so drink a lot because I feel like a lot of the toxins will come out of you. When you take a shower, just close your eyes and imagine the water is white light going all over and touching every part of your body. It's almost as if it is putting a white shield and armor around you which is important because you have to keep your immune system strong.

"And I just want to let you know that everything I said today, I have never said before. Each and every healing is different. Not one is the same. And what we heard today is what you needed to hear, here and now. The energy that is being placed in you will never leave you. So, James, what we are going to do now is place God's seal of white light and love up and down your body. What this does is seal in the healing you have received today which allows you to access it at any time and it will always stay with you. I have other words for you, but first we want to thank you for stepping into this room. We want to thank God for what took place and the words that were given during your session.

"I was told just now that as your loved ones step back into this room that God is giving them strength and they are also being healed on their own level as well because that is what you would want for them. So I just want you to know that each and every one of your loved ones here today will be touched and given strength." With that, Jim, his family, Debra, and Sheri hold hands and recite the Lord's Prayer. The session ends.

❧  ❧  ❧

A poem written by Dr. James Veney after his healing session.

My Life in Blue
I sit in a blue chair.
I stare at a blue wall.
I wait to be called to a blue office
Where a physician in a blue shirt
Will tell me how my life will be assessed
Will it be in words, or milliliters of fluid
Or a little piece of what surrounds my brain?
Is it blue too?

I am in a blue mood as they wheel me
To the radiology room.
On a slab with a blue sheet
The surgeon inserts a long blue needle
Into my spinal column and
Draws off twenty milliliters of fluid.

They are sure my lymphoma has spread
To my brain because of the pale blue light
Surrounding it in the MRI.
My options? Chemotherapy in my port
(Blue under my pale skin)
So debilitating it must be done in a hospital
With those blue sheets.
Or chemotherapy injected directly
Into my spinal column with that blue needle.
Or, of course, nothing.
How long will it take to die?

The physician in the blue shirt calls.
We examined the spinal fluid he says.
There is no lymphoma.
There is no cancer of any kind.
You need no treatment.
Suddenly the world is a bright glowing
Beautiful orange.
Orange sun shining through the window pane
Reflecting off table tops and chairs.
Orange.

"Trust me and refuse to worry, for I am your strength and song. Since I am your strength, I can empower you to handle each task as it comes. Because I am your song, I can give you joy as you work alongside me." - Debra and Sheri

# CHAPTER SIX
## DEEP DEPRESSION

### Rebecca Thomas Healing Session
### January 30, 2013

When Rebecca walked in to The Logos Center the day of her healing, she was in deep despair and no longer wanted to live. When Debra and Sheri first saw her they knew how serious the situation was. Her face and eyes revealed that she was very fragile. It was obvious by her thin frame that she hadn't been eating.

She had come this day asking Debra and Sheri to take her to God because she felt she had lost all hope. She felt that she wanted to die that day. She had even written a note to her husband that morning because she didn't know if she would return home. All she could see was darkness around her and her inner light was no longer shining. She felt helpless and paralyzed. As a counselor, Rebecca had taken all the proper steps for someone in her situation: seeing her own counselor on a weekly basis and taking prescribed antidepressants and sleep medications. Debra and Sheri knew that God was the only one who could heal her.

The Healing Session
Debra begins, "So your job is to receive and just lie there and listen to what God has to say. Follow the steps because I will guide you. I will be holding your hand the entire time and Sheri will be sending you God's healing energy. This is an

experience and a journey and a healing that will never, ever leave you. Now what we are going to do is I have to go through the pain you are experiencing. It is because God is showing me that this is real and in order to heal, we have to feel. So I have to feel it so you never have to. It is okay; it is part of the healing. It is part of the journey.

"Right now what we want to do, Rebecca, is give you some energy, to be able to receive and to be able to have the strength to hear what you are going to hear. We are going to place God's white light and love inside you so you can have the strength, because right now you are depleted."

While Sheri sends Rebecca energy to help her to relax, Debra says, "Now Rebecca, when I start talking, because they are not my words, I do not want you to speak because I want you to receive. If you question or speak, I get out of that zone, so then I have to come back into it. So I just want you to relax your mind and when we are all done, then you can share everything, your experience with us, because we want to hear it. I am going to start the journey, start the words; you are just going to receive it. You do not have to explain anything to me, as God knows everything. You just need to listen. I want you to hear these words. Take a couple of deep breaths, Rebecca, and receive this energy.

"It is getting very cold in this room because there are a lot of loved ones in spirit and they are here to show you that they have your back. Do not feel you are alone. All of these loved ones are coming and they are saying, 'We are here, we are all right here. Don't forget about us. You have our pictures all over your house.' I feel like it is a mother figure coming through saying, 'You have all our pictures in your house, but don't forget we are here. We have your back, we have your back.'

"These words that are coming through right now is God saying you are missing what you have right in front of you. Your husband stands strong with you. Sometimes the others do not fit, but we cannot ignore what we already have. You need to embrace that, hold that, and honor that because it is being given to you through God. He was given to you from God. If you two were the only two left to stand side by side, then that should be enough because God gave you him and in him is God.

"And you are forgetting the most important thing is you. You are forgetting about yourself. What about you? What about you? It's your journey. We are going to start working on the heart chakra because I feel like there have been some daggers put in your heart, things that have been said that have hurt so much that the mind cannot forget. So when we take these out, it can be really painful because there is so much hurt there. But you no longer need to hold it. You no longer need it, you no longer need to own it because whoever voiced it to you, that was their pain they put into you and shame on them for making you hold it.

"So with this first one, which I feel like comes from a mother, we need to pull and as we pull it out it is going to hurt. You are going to cry, it is going to hurt because what we are giving back those words to God. You need to say, 'I don't want to hold it. I don't want to feel guilty. I don't want this anymore. I don't need it. I am going to take this out and I am not going to feel that pain anymore. I am not going to allow this to happen. I am not going to allow this to be part of who I am. I want to live my journey without feeling this guilt about not being the person they want me to be.' We are pulling it out. It is going to hurt. See, you don't want it to go because you take everything on. You are really resisting releasing this.

"This is not yours, Rebecca, this is not yours, and you cannot fix it. This is not up to you to fix. You have to allow this to be taken out. You resist it because you feel like this was your fault. This is not your fault and you need to stop and allow this to come out because I can feel this resistance. Okay, here we go, it is coming out. If it makes you cry, it means you are allowing it to come out too. It's okay, it is coming out slowly, slowly, slowly, slowly. And that one is now out. I feel there are three total and that was the first. The second one is almost like it has been stabbed in the center of your chest and it almost makes it hard for you to breathe or speak, it hurts that bad. But we want to give you your life back and we want to remove this one. This is the pain of all pains because it is holding you back from speaking your truth.

"We are going to take this one out and it is really big. Just imagine the sword and the stone. We are going to release this. We are going to take this one out. This one feels like it has been twisted. You have to allow this to be taken out. Do not hold on to this. You do not deserve this pain. Allow God to take this from you now. Once we take these away you can then have your conversation with God. We have to heal this first. Allow God to take this away. You don't need this pain, you don't need it. You are so stubborn; God says you are stubborn because you want to fix it all. That is why it hurts that much because this is something you can't fix. This is also stronger than what we are, so I am asking God to come in and release whatever is holding this. It needs to be released now and I am asking that God help us to get this out now. I am asking that it is released and taken up to God so that you don't feel it. It is going to be surrendered now."

Debra lets out a moan of pain and agony and says, "It is heavier than heavy, Sheri, and we are not able to lift it." Sheri says she can feel the resistance too as she is trying to pull the dagger out of Rebecca. And Debra says, "This is everything that encompasses you and this is what is happening to you. This is what is going on in you. This is all of your pain sitting right here. This is so heavy and is heavier than anything we know. And I am asking that this be taken off now."

Debra feels it and says, "Ugh, come on!" Debra moans in pain as she feels Rebecca's bad feelings trying to be released. Debra says the daggers do not want to go and compares them to the weight of a heavy rock. It takes everything she has to lift it with Sheri. Finally Debra says the weight has been raised high enough for them to try to lift it from the bottom. Sheri pulls and lifts the weight one more time. Debra, dizzy from pain, moans loudly and announces, "It is gone!"

Debra is out of breath and can barely speak. "When we are so down and we are taken to our deepest depths, that is when we don't see the light. That is when the darkest of darks are placed upon us and that was what was just on you. We asked in the name of God and Jesus Christ to take this away from you and we couldn't have done this without them. They came down and commanded it to be released so that you can see the light right now. You were not seeing the light. You wanted to leave this world because you thought this world wanted you to leave. It was bigger than you. This was not you. The only way this could have been released from you is by God. And that is what was making you feel like this. It was so heavy that you couldn't see beyond it and now that it is gone you can see the light. Do you remember that I am one with you, we are connected, we are together and there is nothing to fear?

"I need you to feel this love and its pure intent. You may feel a little weightless right now because what was on you was so heavy; this weightlessness is a sense of peace. And this peace is God's love. Through a series of breaths we open the third eye, which is in your forehead area between your eyes. I am going to ask that you come out in spirit and take a walk with me. We are going to leave your shell here, your physical body here, and you and I are going to take a journey. You are beyond ready to do this.

"Okay, so you are ready but know this, Rebecca. You are coming back. We are just going here for a moment because we are going to have a conversation with God." Debra gets very cold and tells Rebecca that there are a lot of loved ones surrounding her. "While we are taking this journey, Sheri is going to keep us both anchored here and is going to infuse you with warmth and with God's love.

"I am now standing in front of you in spirit and I am holding your hands. I am looking at you and I know you trust me and I trust you. We are doing this out of love, but when we do this, you are trusting me to take you to a place that you have never been before. I am also trusting you that you are coming back as a new person. You will be the same Rebecca, but renewed."

Rebecca nods her head and gives Debra her word. Debra continues, "With that, I have your permission and what we do is we start floating up after a series of three breaths. Going up, going up, going up." Debra and Rebecca's spirits walk hand in hand.

Debra says, "Imagine a tunnel, like a tube; we are weightless and we are able to go up this tube. We are going up. We are going up, up, up, this tube. Now we step out of this tube and we are onto this platform. We are at a certain level and are going to stay at this level. God says I have to stop at level seven with you, Rebecca. Seven means you will not go to the level where there is the veil. You are going to a level where God can come down to you, but you don't need to go all the way up. It is that level where I have been told that you are safe. You are safe and you will not cross over at this level. You are not allowed to go any higher and God is putting His foot down on that. There may be a day where you can, but on this day you can't. He is going to greet us at this level.

"You may be wondering, 'Why can God come to level seven and why can't I come up to the top?' That is because He is keeping you safe. We see visions of Him all the time so He is at all levels, but He is going to greet you today at this level because this is the level He chose to have a connection with you. So as we stand and wait, you kind of look around and it's almost as if we are standing on a cliff of a mountain. It is beautiful. I see birds. I see sky. It is beautiful and the blue in the sky is like a blue we have never seen before. I want you just to take this all in. We are standing on a mountain, ready to meet God, and it is beautiful. No one else is here; it is just us. The sky is so blue and here comes the white light. It looks like it is just the sun that is beaming down on us, but it is a different type of white light. It is white that looks like the sun, but it is coming from above and it is coming down and it is getting bigger and whiter and whiter. That is God's presence. He is coming down to join us as He places His feet down.

"And you, Rebecca, just fell to your knees. You put your head on His robe and He went down on His knees and He put His arms on your back to hold you. God says, 'It is okay, it is okay.' And you are telling God, 'I can't take this anymore. I can't stand in this light anymore, I can't do it.' God says, 'It is okay, child, it is okay, I have my arms around you. And at this time I just want you to stay.'"

Debra takes a deep breath and says, "Just allow God to hold you. God says it is okay to feel like you can't stand in His light. You feel like you should be standing and are thinking, *Oh my gosh, I should be standing in front of God and honoring Him, but I just can't.*' It is okay, just allow God to embrace you because it feels so good." Debra relays to Rebecca what she is being told that Rebecca is feeling: "I feel loved, I feel good. I like this feeling. Now I know I don't have to worry. I just feel okay. I feel loved and for once I feel like I am at a place where I don't have to think about it. I like this. I almost see your body staying there and you are crying in this little ball. I feel like your spirit is coming out and you are holding God's hand. He is looking at you and you are looking at Him eye to eye. You don't see anything but His eyes.

"God says to you, 'Dear child, you do not need to hold on to this. This is not yours to hold on to. You need to be who it is that I made you to be.' Don't become someone they want you to be just for acceptance. Your intentions were pure. If they choose not to see it, it is not your fault. It is their loss and it is their journey, not yours. It is only hurting them more because you are a beautiful, beautiful being. You always come from love in everything that you do and if somebody wants to destroy this fragile person, then you cannot allow them to break you and shatter you. What they do has nothing to do with who you are. God knows the truth.

"Sometimes when things like this happen and relationships are severed and families go in other directions, we are left alone and we feel abandoned. We need to use that time to discover why God is putting you here all alone. Why are you being removed from everyone else? Because there is a purpose and reason for this and you will see this through these lessons that are happening all around you, affecting you in every way. And you have helped so many people before and can't help yourself.

"It is through this lesson that you will see how it all plays out. I see that you are writing. I see writing and you need to write and maybe this will help. Put it in a form so that if you never get to vocalize it, it will be on paper; it will have been voiced. Maybe it will take reading your book for them to understand who you are and what just took place and all the pain that was put on you. It is like self-healing as it not only heals you, it heals them when they are ready to read it. And then at that point, God says you are releasing it. Stand in your light. Stand in your truth. Stand with your husband. Be one together. Have this time together. Don't look at it as a hurtful time. Take this time for yourself. I am giving it to you.

"Do the things you have never been able to do before. And if those who are around you, whom you are missing so much, can't be part of it, then they are the ones missing out, not you. When you keep the door open, even if it is only a crack, they will find their way through it. But now you have to let go of the control because it isn't the way you want it to be. It doesn't mean that it is not the right way because this is God's way and things are going to play out the way they need to. You need to know that God has a purpose for you. This is where you need to be right now.

"The stomach area does hurt because I can feel it. You are not eating and it hurts when you eat. It hurts when you eat because you want to die. This is not okay, not okay. This isn't the way that one dies. I am going to heal this stomach area and it is going to take a little work." Sheri places energy in Rebecca's stomach area with her palms. "Damage has been done so it hurts now to digest food. It hurts because your mind and your brain are thinking, *When I eat, I hurt, and if I don't eat, I will feel better because I get to go to God.* We need to rewire her brain to not think that way. We need to rewire it so when she eats, the stomach no longer feels pain. The whole stomach area needs to be healed.

"You stand in front of me and you look at me and I look at you. You look over to the left and you see your body on the floor in a ball, not able to stand, not able to walk, not able to even eat. And I look at you spirit to spirit, eye to eye. And God says, 'I want you to look at your shell sitting on the floor, and I want you to know that this shell is my gift that I gave you and that gift is called life. I gave you the gift of life and some things are going to be hard, but when you have me and you know that I am in you and you are in me, you can accomplish anything.' Just know that God sees the bigger picture. Right now you are in a dust storm and you can't see at all. It is okay. God has you, He is holding you, and he will never leave you. He sees the big picture and you need to trust that.

"You need to let the worry go. You need to just be. Remember the gift God gave you: LIFE. You are forgetting all the moments that are just about sitting and having your coffee or tea. Enjoy it! Do not let this age you. Do not let this suffocate you. Do not let this haunt you. Do not let this stop you from eating and receiving life. Shame on them, shame on them. This pain is so deep it's as if someone came in and did the worst possible thing. God is telling you that He is giving you permission not to hold it, but to enjoy life because He gave you life. You are a part of Him, you are a fragment of Him and He wants you to enjoy it. He gave this to you. So take these moments and enjoy them. Everything is going to be okay because God is holding it and you are no longer holding it and He is going to make it work. God is holding it now, you are not.

"Do not worry about other family members. Do not ever think they will forget about you or that they forget that you love them. It is through your prayers that God makes sure they receive it. I am hearing you say, 'When will I be with them again?' Maybe in time. I don't know when that time is but right now you are standing in front of your Almighty Father and I am telling you that this is your journey. This is what you need to do. By praying, they receive it. They know who you are; they have never stopped feeling your love. That is your purpose right now. Your purpose is to love yourself. You need to feel that you deserve this life. So when we heal your heart, we are also placing God's white light inside your body so you feel that you deserve love. You are blessed!

"Without God, you would fall. But now you are not going to fall because you have God. He holds you and is not going to let you go. You start feeling God in yourself every day. When you wake up, walk with Him, breathe with Him and start living. If you wake up with Him and walk with Him and breathe with Him, you honor Him, and you are honoring yourself. He loves you and He puts His arms around you right now. He is lifting you up and having your spirit look at that body and saying you are going to go back in that body and stand strong, because I stand strong in you. And at this time you are back inside that body. You still do not want to stand up. You are still feeling a little weak, but you feel so much stronger.

"He lifts you up and He holds you tightly and He says, 'I gave you this gift of life. Honor it. That shell of yours, treat it as a gift. Eat and drink knowing that you have a purpose here.'

The thought of leaving disservices you because you will feel guilty up here, looking down, and you will say, 'Why did I go?' What happens if things were to change? You would want to come back and you couldn't.

"Life is fragile and you need to treat it as such. You do not want to shatter it because you only get one. You shatter it and you may regret it because you do not know what lies ahead. So don't always look at the worst. Look at things as a blessing. This may seem like the worst thing that is happening, but treat it as a blessing of time. This blessing of time is giving you time to now work on yourself and to enjoy the time as a couple with your husband. Do the things you never got to do before. And maybe people will start to say, 'Wow, they are so happy, I want to be part of that.'

"God is giving you permission to be happy again. You need to honor that. Do not let family allow you to feel the blame and then feel the pain. No, the daggers have been taken out, they are gone. So just stand here and feel the embrace of God."

Debra adds, "My stomach is really hurting, they must be really working on this area. They are working on the intestines area. As God is embracing you right now, I want you to feel this warmth. I want you to take in this love because it will never leave you. I want you to know that God is telling you that you have a purpose and your mission is not over. You are not on borrowed time, Rebecca, you have lots of time. You need to go honor that time and make the best of it because it is a gift. Climb the tallest mountain. Go to a beach. You are now standing tall. You can feel it and you know it.

"Sheri has been giving healing energy to your entire body during this time. I want you to relax while you are still in a space where you are out of body, but still in the body, as they continue to work on the stomach area." Debra moans in pain as the spiritual doctors continue working. "I feel like they are reconstructing your linings. They have filled this area with a lot of fluids. Be gentle to yourself today. Eat, sleep, and let this all heal as if you just had real surgery. At this time I want you to come back into your body. You can just feel yourself inside again and you can feel your shoulders again. We will now do the seven seals of God's white light and love and finish the healing."

Sheri says, "Your whole body was cleansed and purified. There was so much energy going through me to you and your whole body was infused with pure love and God's light. Your body was also realigned and rebalanced for you to stand strong. Remember that you carried a huge weight so that was lifted. When we take something so heavy off you, you might be really tired. Sometimes people feel like they just want to go home and cry. You might just go home and feel this new joy that you didn't have before. It is unexplainable and it is stronger than who you are."

After her healing session, Debra and Sheri can tell that Rebecca radiates a glow of peace. When asked about it, Rebecca says, "I can't explain it, but I feel it."

⚜ ⚜ ⚜

When Rebecca arrived at the healing session, Debra and Sheri could see that she was physically weighed down with despair. But after hearing God's words, Rebecca's light within glowed again. A woman who had been in The Logos Center during Rebecca's healing saw her transformation and remarked, "Wow, what just happened to that lady? She went in with her head down and hopeless, and now she leaves with hope."

"I heal many through one." - Debra and Sheri

# CHAPTER SEVEN
# EMBRACING SELF-WORTH AND
# SELF-LOVE

**Yvonne Divel Healing Session**
**January 30, 2013**

Yvonne Divel, who is Sheri's sister, was visiting Arizona from Missoula, Montana. She has one son and one grand-daughter whom she adores.

Yvonne's faith is very strong. She reads the Bible every day to maintain her connection with God. At the time of her healing, she was debating whether or not to continue a serious relationship. Actually, Yvonne was questioning much in her life like her career and her life plan in general. It was this uncertainty that led her to request a healing session with Debra and Sheri. Though Debra had met Yvonne briefly years ago, all Debra knew was that Yvonne was experiencing major stomach issues and that is why she came for a healing.

In this healing there were specific details that Debra gave to Yvonne that Sheri really questioned; after all, she knew her sister better than anyone and God's message did not seem to make any sense. However, God's presence in the room was overwhelming and the feeling of love was undeniable; therefore, Sheri realized that she could not question these words coming through Debra for Yvonne. The message made sense only to Yvonne, as she had not shared this painful deep secret with anyone. Yvonne was speechless and cried during the session. She was not expecting this information to come through; she felt she had already dealt with it on her own.

The Healing Session

Debra begins, "Our journey begins right here, Yvonne. We are being directed by God and you can see the power of God working through me and Sheri in different ways." Debra stands at the foot of the table, holding Yvonne's ankles, and she begins to feel excruciating pain in her lower right side/ abdomen area. In her mind, Debra sees surgeons coming in right away and feels urgency. Debra knows these are doctors by their appearance: They have surgical masks, latex gloves, and surgical instruments. Debra then positions herself under the table to become one with Yvonne and starts speaking.

"When I was standing at the end of the table, I was feeling like this is urgent and needs to be done now. So I see these doctors and I can feel a bump in my abdomen area and the pain is killing me. I just want you to close your eyes and the doctors are coming in right now and they are going to heal this area. I see two doctors. One is going to oversee the work and one is going to do the work. One is on the right side of you now and it is really cold in here all of a sudden. I feel like there are a lot of loved ones here too, watching over you. I don't know where this little girl is coming from, but I see a little girl here as well. They are telling me we need to do the surgery right now but I wanted to describe to you everything that I was seeing."

Medicine is now being administered; Debra tastes it and feels it in her nose. "I see about a three-inch incision being made on your right side. This problem might also give you a little acid reflux at times. They will work on this area to the right side of the abdomen and also above your belly button." Debra breathes hard as they work on this area. "They are going in here and I hear the word 'suction.' They are going to suction something out and I also feel pinching. They just pinched a needle in there. As the needle goes in you, they must be extracting something. They are taking something out. I just felt a piercing and felt the needle go way in. There is something that is not working properly in here.

"I feel like they are going in and they are snipping. That needle went in to extract everything that was inside there. They are opening up a valve in this area." Debra cries out in pain. She is dizzy and feels like she is going to throw up. A large dose of medicine is administered. "I feel like all the acids are coming upwards as they push down there. I can taste it in my throat. The valve has been opened, the valve has been opened. This is an intense surgery. This isn't something that is just a scope. It is bigger and it goes down to the deepest area that they are going to open up. So yes, it can be done but it is dangerous surgery, meaning that it could have major complications. I am hearing just because we do this doesn't mean you should stop taking all of your other medications. They go together.

"I am all of a sudden getting a little migraine headache in my right eye. I don't know if you experience these light headaches in your temples—it must all go together. You are going to need to be very careful what you eat and what you put in to your body because this is very major what you did today. Very major!

"When you step out of this room, it will be good for you to go and sleep. They are opening your third eye because you are questioning all the time and saying to God, 'Tell me and I will do it, I will listen.' Your faith is strong, but you do question. You are hearing it, but now you want to see it. You say, 'Show me, God, show me through my third eye so that I feel safe, so that I know what I am doing is just not in my mind but that I know what I need to do.' There are many things that need to be done. You have too much going on in your life. It is very cluttered. You need to have this cleared. You need to remove yourself from all this clutter because that's what is holding you down. That is what is causing some of the pain inside, because you are devaluing who you are.

"You are not soaring to your ability. So it is now time to clear your clutter. So now the third eye is being opened so that you have the ability to see it now. It doesn't mean the vision comes right away, it doesn't mean you sit down and the vision is right there. Sometimes it will come when you least expect it or it will come in a dream and that is when you really know that you are not just making it up. It comes so loud and so clear and that is what also gives you strength to see and know what you need to do. You know it was given to you and you know it is not yours.

"There is someone standing at the top of your head who is holding you and loving you. It is a loved one letting you know that he or she is here. There is someone touching your hair.

"I am going to go back to this little girl who came into the room at the beginning of your session. I don't know what age this happened but for some reason I feel there is a little girl who passed. Maybe you had a miscarriage. Maybe you didn't know you had one and she was going to come but she didn't? Maybe there was a time you thought you were pregnant but you ended up not being pregnant? That is because God changed the plan for you. I do see that the little one who is here for you, she is yours. She chose not to be here on this planet, but she is yours on the other side. I am going to take you on a spiritual journey and you are going to meet this little girl. We are going to push your spirit out of your third eye and you will know and will see her."

Yvonne is overcome with emotion and breaks down crying. Debra soothes, "I just want you to calm down as there are no worries and you are not going to think. You are going to move the mind away and I want you to just close your eyes and really, really, really relax. I want you to take a deep breath and just relax everything that is within you. It just feels so good that I am lying on this table, so relaxed and calm. I feel safe and I know God is here and that He is taking care of me. There is nothing for me to fear and I am just relaxing.

"Another deep breath. And when you take that deep breath you are ready to take another breath in. That is when the spirit comes out. I am going to take your hand and your spirit will be out. So just concentrate on the spirit coming out. Very good, you are almost out and there you go—you are out. Just relax; we are just in this room, not anywhere else. I am holding your hand. Don't think, don't move, just be. We are standing together in spirit and you have a big smile and a look like, 'This is kind of freaky.' You are holding my hand and your spirit can see your body lying right there on the table.

"So we are still in this room and what I want to do now is almost like flying. It is like we are looking at the light and we are pushing our hands down and as we do, we are pushing and getting higher and higher and higher and higher. We are being lifted and going through that hole. Remember the white light coming through the top of the pyramid. We are going up to that white light and we are going higher. We are feeling weightless as we go higher and all of a sudden we are feeling lighter and lighter. You are holding my hand so we are safe. We are taking a journey, a fun experience. Now we are really up there. We are really to the space where we are weightless and now we are at this level where we are going to walk forward. So we do not need to go any higher.

"We are holding hands and we are just kind of walking forward to the white light. There are no expectations. And there is the little girl. I am standing to your left and I am holding your hand and as you look down to your right, there is this cute little girl. Cute, cute, cute. She looks like she is about four years old and she is looking at you. I just heard her say, 'Mommy, Mommy.' And you are looking at her and saying, 'She is really mine? Is she really mine? Wow!'

"You pick her up and she wraps her legs around your waist and the two of you are now looking face to face. And you know right now she is yours, she looks so much like you that there is no denying that she is yours. And there is no reason to feel guilty for anything because she is here now showing you, 'I have always been here for you, Mom.' So now you put her down. She kind of went off to the right because she is going to stay there as we walk forward. She is not going to walk with us. She is probably going to see us as we journey back, but this is kind of like her area, her play area. She is going to stay there. She is just smiling and beaming as if to say, 'I am so proud of my mom.'"

While Debra and Yvonne take this journey, Yvonne's body is being worked on by Sheri and the spiritual surgeons. Then Debra says, "I am getting pain in my lower back, so now they are working on your lower back and lower kidneys. So now you and I are going to walk forward and we are just going to keep walking and walking."

Debra starts to cry and says, "I am getting very overwhelmed right now because as we get closer and closer, we are getting closer to the Kingdom of Heaven. And I want you to see what I am seeing. I know who I see and I will speak it for you."

Debra breathes deeply and is overwhelmed by what she sees. "I see angels and I see this big pearly gate, this is a beautiful pearly gate. The color is this pearly color that just shimmers and shines. We can't go through that gate, but we are at the gates of heaven.

"So as we are standing at the gate, we see all these angels and we see all of this white light. It is almost like you are seeing this glisten, and when I say glisten, it is like this glittery glistening. It just has this sparkly glow to the light and it is around us. It encompasses us and it is everywhere. We are just going to stand and wait. The gates are not opening. They do not need to open for God or Jesus to appear. If you can just imagine a robe appear. I am seeing the bottom of it as if He is floating from above in front of the gates and coming down, coming down.

"Now we are only seeing hands and from the waist down and we are not seeing shoulders or a face. I am just seeing this huge, huge presence with the robe and the hands that is higher than we are, grander, bigger, larger, than what we are. We feel like children standing there. We can't even look up. Just so much bigger than what we know. The hands are open!"

So Debra tells Yvonne that she is going to let go of her hands. "I want you just to put your hands in His hands. When I say His hands, this is the Almighty. This is your heavenly father. And you are going to place your hands inside so that it is like putting palm to palm in His hands. And when you put your palms on His, He closes His hands around yours. This is going to be overwhelming because you feel this love that encompasses you and you are in the presence of the Almighty Father and you feel so much love. It is beyond what I have ever experienced"-Debra and Sheri are both overwhelmed and crying with God's presence –"so take it in, Yvonne. You are going to speak to Him and He is going to allow you to stay in this light and hold His hands. Even though you are holding His hands and feeling this amount of love, it is effortless.

"It actually feels like He has His arms around you and you are just being embraced. I feel like He just drew you in and He is holding you. All of a sudden I feel like I am being held. He is holding you. And that is what you are missing. You are missing someone to hold you, to tell you that everything is going to be okay. So your Almighty Father came down and He is embracing you and He is not going to let you go and He is saying, 'This is what you are missing. You are not receiving it from your father, your mother, and you did not receive it from your husband.'

"This is what you need, you need to know that someone is holding you, someone loves you, someone hears you, someone is watching over you, someone is guiding you, someone is never going to leave you and this someone is the Almighty Father, your Lord. So as He holds you and as He embraces you, He is giving you something that you have been wanting and He wants you to receive this, knowing that you can have this at any time: this embrace, for it never leaves you, He is always with you. Do not fear this next step in your life. Do not fear, because I have my arms around you. I have my arms around you. Fear holds you down. God holds you up. God will never let you down. Fear holds you down. Fear drags you through the mud. God holds you up. Remember this–fear, detach from it.

"Allow God to hold you, walk through it knowing He holds your hand. He knows what you need. Right now God knows you need this embrace. You need to know you are loved. You are lacking the love and you are not being loved. You are not being loved to the point you need; therefore, because you are not receiving it, you are not loving yourself. This is causing some of the issues you are having right now. He is not letting you go because you are His child and now He is telling you as He is holding you, 'You are not loving yourself. You are worthy, you are worthy.' He wants you to say, 'I am worthy of love.' And now I want you to say what God says: 'God loves me, then

I love myself.' So I want you to say now, I love myself, I love myself, I love everything about myself, I love everything about myself, I love everything about myself.

"Don't say, well, I don't love this part. NO, I love everything about myself. Because God is holding you and remember He is your creator, He made you. So if you think there is a part of you that you don't like, you are telling God that you don't like the way He created you. I don't think we can say that. God says He loves everything about you so now you need to love everything about yourself. God says, 'I created you just the way you are, who you are, how you are, and what you are. And if the person you are with does not love you for who you are, what you are, and all that I created, then you are not being valued.'

"And if you are not being valued, you are not being loved, and when you are not feeling loved you stop loving yourself. You do not have the courage or the strength in life to walk forward because fear takes over. It is time and we are going to cut the cords of fear from you. We are going to cut these cords of fear and you are going to be stronger than ever because God is hanging on to you and He is not letting go.

"I can tell you I have never seen an embrace from God this hard and this long. He is not letting you go until He feels He can cut the fear from you and give you all this strength that you will not be able to deny. It will be so strong that you will say, 'What the heck is wrong with me, even if I want to I cannot fear it. I cannot *not* move forward because God is within me now and He's the one who is doing the walk.' So if you feel weak, just say, 'God, walk for me, God walk for me.' He is still embracing you. He is not going to let you go because you are still fragile and He wants to make sure you know that you are loved. You are loved.

"And this didn't just come overnight, this is something that didn't just happen. This is years and years and years from everything building up in you. In fact, that little girl reminded me of you. Things just built up. This has happened from when you were little and just kept building and building and that's why you receive the people you receive in your life, because you feel abandoned, you don't feel the love. You don't know what real love is like. You don't know how to accept it. You don't know how to see it. But now you know how to feel it because God has infused you with love and you won't deny the right love, but you won't accept the wrong love anymore.

"We cut all of these cords that are from the past. They are from all the pain of feeling like you were not loved. And you may question why you felt it but did not receive it. It was no one's fault, it is just part of life. You don't need to put blame or question why. All we need to know is what is taking place right now. So God is saying, don't go back later and think, hmm, when did all this begin? Don't go and do that because then you are bringing it all back and we are releasing it right now. We are releasing that so you can move forward. If you go backwards, then you are bringing those feelings back on.

"Right now you are in the presence of God and being held and He is saying that He is releasing you from head to toe. Feel it, receive it. 'I am worthy of love. God loves me.' I want you to repeat what I say in your mind. 'I feel God's love right now. God loves me. God loves me. God holds me. This feeling will never leave me. As I feel the love of God then I know I am worthy of love. I am worthy of love. I love myself.'

"When God gives His love, He is not only just putting love in you, He is putting Himself in you. You are becoming one, so if you love thy Father, you love thy one. It is easier to say, 'I love myself because I know I am one with God.' That is a lot easier and has a much deeper meaning.

"God is going to give you one more big squeeze and then He is going to step back. He is holding your hand now and He is saying, 'Know that I will never leave you, know that I am one step ahead of you, know that I know what you need and what is best.' You hear it, you know it, but you don't want to walk it, because you are a little frightened and that is okay. Don't let the fear hold you back.

"God has left and now I am stepping forward and I am going to hold your hand and you see the pearly gates and you are like, 'Wow!' There will be a day when you walk through those gates because when you pass, the gates will be open.

"You are seeing the little girl again. She is not coming to us, she is just standing there and you are now going to come back into the room slowly, slowly, slowly. We are coming back into our bodies. While you were on your journey, the surgeons were working on you, fixing the abdomen area and sewing you up. You will be sore in your lower right back and kidney area. Just drink lots of water, as toxins will continue to come out. You will be tired as you had major surgery. At this time Sheri will seal the healing with God's white light and love."

## Words from God

"Trust is the biggest key. I hold your hands very firmly; trust in me. You do not need anyone but me. If someone does not adore you, he does not deserve you. Do not stay out of fear. Walk forward knowing I am holding your hands and then all will be well and the burdens will lift from you."

"All of my children need to be adored, respected, honored, and loved. When they are not, they need to seek something different. And all of my children need to honor, respect, adore, and love themselves because if they can honor, adore, respect, and love themselves, they will never accept any less than that from another person."

"So as you walk forward, this is the work that needs to be done. For when you teach this to yourself, when you go within and you learn that the power comes from me, when you learn that you can love, respect, and adore yourself stand strong, you are teaching your own children to love, adore, and respect themselves."

"That is what each of my children should know because if they can feel that inside where they love themselves like I love them, then they are able to handle and go through anything because nothing else matters. They are just burdens that come down your path. You can't help others until you take care of yourself. All is well. All is well."

# CHAPTER EIGHT
# FACING ADDICTION AND RECOVERY
# EMERGENCY DISTANT HEALING

**Kenneth Paul Bridwell Healing Session**
**April 6, 2013**

Kenneth Bridwell was a happy, healthy child who grew up in Arizona. As he got older, he nurtured compassion toward people and animals. Tall, smart, and handsome, Kenneth impressed his teachers with his maturity and it seemed as if the world was his for the taking.

Kenneth's family noticed a change in him during his sophomore year of high school. He began lying and stealing and grew distant from friends and family. Soon it became clear that Kenneth had started using drugs. What started as abuse of prescription drugs morphed into full-fledged addiction to heroin.

On April 6, 2013, seventeen-year-old Kenneth was assaulted by another young man and suffered a traumatic brain injury that almost cost him his life. Hemorrhaging in his brain was likely to lead to severe brain damage or death.

Kenneth's mother, Jennifer, made a desperate call to Debra. She had heard that Debra and Sheri performed distance healings with just the name and a photo of a person. She told Debra that her son had been attacked and was in the hospital. Debra sent Sheri the photo of Kenneth that his mother had sent via text. Both women felt an immediate connection to Kenneth and they quickly set out for the healing room at The Logos Center.

Sheri was overcome with tears while driving to the healing as she felt the presence of Mother Mary. She had never experienced anything like that before. What she didn't know was that Jennifer was in the hospital chapel praying to a statue of Mary, calling out for help for her son. Upon arriving at the healing center, Debra and Sheri prayed at the altar before beginning the healing session in the Threshold Room.

The Healing Session

Debra begins, "We have Kenneth Paul Bridwell's picture on the healing table with a cross that says Miracles and a cross that says the Lord's Prayer. To the left of the healing table there is a picture of Jesus." Sheri and Debra hold hands and ask God to use them as His instruments.

Debra says, "I am getting dizzy already. What we will do is I will lie on the table and be Kenneth's proxy and receive what it is that he needs."

Sheri has been praying and sending him energy from the time she received the call that morning. She again feels the presence of Mother Mary and is overcome by tears. Debra lies on the table with Kenneth's picture on top of her abdomen. Immediately her left eye feels swollen.

Debra says they are ready and Mother Mary is a big part of this healing. Then she says, "For some reason I can't let go of Sheri's hands. Sheri is now doing energy work on the left side of my head. I can feel lots of energy going through my temples, especially the right. I am feeling like my jaw is messed up."

Debra feels medicine administered up her nose. "He must have always stood with his hands in his pockets because I have that feeling where I am standing here with my hands in my pockets. I am getting lots of head pressure. My left eye is very swollen like I can't open it. I feel like I want to throw up from all of the meds. They are making me feel that way. They have him so sedated. I just feel like there are so many meds in him that I want to throw up. My head hurts so bad. I can see inside, the swelling.

"And we just want to calm everything inside. It is like putting an ice pack on something when it is swollen and you are just calming that area down. My left cheek hurts too. They may not even know about his cheek yet. The spiritual surgeons are repairing the left cheek. I feel this has happened for a reason and Kenneth will value life now. It was like he was given a second chance and he knows it. And he knows it within.

"I can feel the energy from Sheri, very palpable. It feels like a ball bouncing inside my head. The energy, oh my gosh, is making me dizzy. Everything is being smoothed out. I feel like they are working on the eyes so that he has no vision problems. When I say vision, I mean like a twitch of the eye. They are working on that. So if he does have a twitch of the eye, just know that it will go away. It is just a sign to show you that that was there and it will no longer be.

"I feel what took place was transforming. This accident shifted him to a new person. I feel like he will appreciate life more, which will shift him. He may need to step in here on this table and he will get all his clarity and everything will line up for him. I do see that happening. I still feel it is touch and go, touch and go. I feel like I am connecting with him. I just tasted a bunch of medicine that went in. Blah! My chest feels heavy, my heart could go. I feel touch and go, touch and go, where I want to talk to him. Do not give up. That's what I feel like I need to tell him. Do not give up, because the rest is up to you now. Do not give up!

"I just felt a pinch in my abdomen right at the same time Sheri moved to this area. You know when we do drugs it affects our organs, and I felt it affected down near his liver area. And right when I felt it, Sheri went over and was guided to heal that area. As I was feeling it, she was healing it. And so the damage that had been done with the other drugs he put in his body is being healed right now so that he can be strong and allow this healing to take place. So they are putting his organs and everything inside back to its original state. And it is something over here, like the liver, kidneys. I can really feel all of them in that area bloating up. As you're putting the energy on them, I can feel them moving. It is odd that the organs are moving. I can feel them being touched and healed and sealed with God's love and healing.

"In order for the body to heal, everything has to be working in sync. And although the doctors in the hospital worked on the brain, they put a lot of meds in him, which could cause other things to fail. So we are here to make sure all his other organs that were somewhat damaged are healed so that he can heal. It is really important that they keep his neck straight. I almost feel like they need to put a neck brace on him so when he wakes up and tries to turn his head, it will keep his neck straight. Please keep it straight. It needs to be straight.

"This was all about timing. Everything else in his body needed to be realigned or he wouldn't have had the full strength. My ear is hurting. I feel he could be having a conversation with God right now. Wow, I actually see Kenneth watching us in this room, and he stands at the end of this table. He knows something is taking place. He feels it and knows it and I can see him standing right there, accepting it. He is in awe.

"I have so many chills right now, Sheri. Oh my gosh, he looks much younger than his picture and he is just looking at what is being done and is in awe. Oh, this really hurts and I hope nothing in this abdomen area is giving out on him right now. He is in deep pain and is breathing very deeply with labored breathing. We have to fix that." Debra sees that Kenneth has to return to his body. She then screams out in tremendous pain. "Thank goodness they are working on this area right here, it feels like the kidney, it goes straight through. They are taking the toxins out that have been in his body for a while. I can feel it coming out through my solar plexus/belly button area. These are all cords from attachments of making him want this and need it and they are all going to be released so that he doesn't want this or need this anymore, as far as addiction goes." Debra is in extreme pain as all of the toxins are being removed. "Kenneth will be fine. I just felt such coldness when I said this.

"There are so many loved ones here for him, and angels. And they surround this room in glory. He has angels here standing next to him and also at his bedside, angels watching over him. I see two, one on his left side and one by his head. They will reside with him this entire time. Kenneth is still standing here."

Debra asks, "Am I missing something, because he is still standing there? He is just watching and I feel like he has a choice. And they are cleansing his organs so they do not fail on him. Oh, I just saw the hospital monitors. Maybe they had a glitch while we were here. But I just saw the monitors go stable. He is stable, he is stable. I feel like he put his hand in my hand to say, 'I am good.' He cupped his hand like a shake of gratitude. I still feel the healing going into the right side of my abdomen and all that area. It is the kidneys.

"When Sheri realigns all the meridians and all the strands, that balances him emotionally, physically, spiritually. His body, mind, and soul are being rejuvenated and it is like he is being reborn. Everything is being put back in alignment from head to toe."

Sheri says, "Wow, this energy is so strong."

Debra continues, "I have my body totally straight with my hands up above my head. I feel like I am being stretched. Sheri is aligning the body from head to toe, inside and out, body, mind, and soul."

Sheri says, "My arm actually aches because there is much energy going through it."

Debra says, "Oh, I can feel you pulling, all the little strands are moving straight. I can still smell that everything is so sterile in the hospital room. It is almost like ammonia. I can smell that. I feel the strands from my knees all the way up, almost as if I am being infused with all this light. It is God's energy that is being infused inside the body–every vessel, every organ, every vein, all the blood, all the cells. I can feel them all being filled up. I feel like everything is swelling. But don't be alarmed if he is swelling because he is just being infused with the healing and the energy and the light and love. I feel like his knees and his legs are swollen. It is okay. I still have a little pain in my right side but think this is just normal because of the work that I just went through.

"Actually, when Sheri started working in the stomach area, I was feeling a pinching and now I am feeling it being infused with this energy where it feels like, almost like if you imagine bandaging that area. I do still smell that ammonia in the hospital room. This smell is very strong and is really bothering me. I would really like it if Kenneth's mom were able to put a different fragrance in the room because Kenneth does not like this smell. They could even get some lavender oil. They can just place it under his nose. And now I am being told the healing is complete."

Sheri asks if Kenneth left. Debra says, "Yes. Everything was touch and go, but I don't feel it is anymore because I felt like he was here and there, here and there. One moment he was just watching and then he gave us the handshake to say thank you. He was having to make a choice. And he wouldn't have had the choice if we hadn't given him the healing on the kidneys and the organs. So what we thought we were coming to heal–the head–we ended up healing something totally different.

Sheri places one more beam of energy through the top of the head that will go all the way down through the body. And Debra says, "I can feel it. Envision the top of the head opening up and the white light is going all the way through, like pounding it through, so there is not any part of his energy that is not receiving this light. This is the love of God. He will be forever changed. Now I feel like they are sprinkling holy water over every part of him. It infuses the mind, body, spirit, and soul in holiness, protecting it, sealing it, healing it, emotionally, physically, and spiritually inside and out. Every healing is different and this one is special in its own right."

Sheri and Debra hold hands as they say the Lord's Prayer together. They give thanks to God, Jesus, Mother Mary, all the angels, the surgeons, Kenneth, and his mother for giving them permission to perform the healing. It is so peaceful in the room that Debra and Sheri don't want to leave.

# Chapter Nine

# God Speaks to Kenneth

## Kenneth Paul Bridwell
## Second Healing Session
## April 26, 2013

Kenneth and his family wanted to meet Debra and Sheri and see the room where the healing had taken place. This was the first time they all had met but it felt like greeting friends after a long separation. They all shared an instant bond of pure love.

Debra and Sheri spontaneously felt it would be powerful if Kenneth would have his own experience on the healing table to feel the power and the presence of God. They wanted to give Kenneth the opportunity to have God speak to him.

The Healing Session
Kenneth lies on the healing table and Debra arranges herself underneath the table to become one with him so that she can see what it is that he needs.

Debra says, "Imagine this as a really fun ride. That is what I am being told to tell you. Immediately I feel coldness in the room, so what is happening is that loved ones are joining us, and your mother's friend is here. She is standing over to the right and behind you, saying thank you because ultimately it was your choice to come back or not. I feel the presence of God, our Father, in this room. So what is happening is that I want you to close your eyes and take a series of three breaths. I will do this with you.

"I am going to guide you on a spiritual journey. This is just going to calm us. You are going to take your first big breath now. Take it in and let it out. I feel a little more weightless, calmer, and very relaxed. And as you relax, I want you to envision right now God, but you can't see His face. But you can see His beautiful robe and He is standing in front of you and you can see His hands. I want you to envision that you are standing next to Him. Sometimes it is hard to see ourselves, so feel yourself standing next to Him. You look at Him and you recognize the face for it looks a lot like Jesus. And you connect with the eyes and now you remember that you once stood here before. And you once were looking down on your body being operated on. And you stood next to God like you are doing now.

"There are many, many choices that you were given and you were very thorough. You went down through these choices and you answered. One of the choices was, do you want to come back, and do you want to live? You questioned it to make sure what form your body would take if you came back and God said, 'I will give you back the body you once had.' Then God asked if you would rather go back and have a simpler life, but one where you would no longer need a brain. And you stood there and you thought for a while and then you answered, 'I want to go back to my original state.' With that, God asked you the next question. 'Do you want to go back to the original state or a shifted state of your conscious mind?' And you didn't know what that meant. And He said, 'Do you want to go back to the original state to have the cravings and the need to continue on the path that you were once walking? Or do you want a shift to take place that will take you on my path, which is knowing and speaking that I am your Lord?' And you said, 'The shifted.'

"At that time you looked down at your body and it looked as if there was this white tornado that was being infused from your head to your toes and it was encompassing all around you and you were going, 'Wow, what is taking place?' It looked like a dream where it encompassed everything inside of you, every cell, every organ. It was touching inside, yet you could see it surrounding you on the outside. What was this? This was God's touch; this was God's white light. This was God that encompassed you inside and out, putting you back in perfect form, to walk this new walk. At the same time you were given strength, the strength of being able to say no and the strength to be able to walk away from those who seemed to be friends. God was giving you the strength, for you were the one who made the decision to go on the right path.

"All your cravings and old habits were removed when you were infused with that white light. So looking down, you couldn't wait to get back. You were full of laughter standing there in spirit. And when you came into this room to see that we were healers and healing you, you were smiling, knowing that all has been done already. So why were we doing it?

"Because it was through our hands and through our words that God placed this white light inside you. And if that hadn't taken place, you wouldn't have had the conversation you had with God. Everything was aligned, and the power allowed you to stay on a realm to have a conversation with God. So God stands in this room to tell you the consequences of what we do, and so does your mom's friend who stands here saying this as well by nodding her head, as she is hearing these words.

"Our choices that we make in life all have consequences that can lead to how we pass. So honor your body as if it is a gift. A gift from God, very fragile, like a piece of glass that if it were to fall, it would shatter. So on this new path, watch all of your choices because they all have consequences and you are only given one life. But in your life you have been given two. And this woman over here keeps shaking her head like, Yes, yes, yes, you better be listening to this because she wasn't given a second chance and you were. It is a lot to comprehend and a lot to take on but when you know the power of feeling when God's presence is in the room and that He is the one who did this work, it is beyond any words that you can explain.

"You now know that He is guiding you and pushing you in this right direction. There is nothing to fear because He is one step ahead of you and if you just know this walking forward, you won't ever fear the next step or think, I can't do this. For if God is leading you, then yes, you can do this. You can have and do whatever it is that you want. Remember, He gave you a choice and you could go back to the old way and you chose not to. That is called free will. But with your free will and the choices you made, He is now the one leading and guiding and holding your hand.

"There is some guilt that you need to have removed from your heart. When you were having the conversation with God, you saw the pain that you put your mother through, and you see it now because you are more aware. It is like you grew up in this shift and you have the guilt of what you did and the pain that you caused. You need to know that you can be released from that guilt because God is not upset with you. Your mother is no longer upset with you and you should not be upset with yourself either, for love is unconditional and those were the choices you made.

"But if you hadn't made those choices, you wouldn't have had this experience. Everything happened the way it was supposed to because this was your outline, this was your life, this was your purpose to change who you were. You made the ultimate sacrifice. But with that we need to release from your heart the guilt so that the bond that you have with your mom is strong. So now we release this guilt and give it to God so you no longer worry or hurt and so your heart can be opened and filled with pure white light and love.

"You learned from it. If you didn't learn from it, you would have to do the lesson over. We don't want to repeat lessons.

We learn from it, we walk away from it, we release it, and at this time we are healed completely. Amen."

Debra asks Kenneth if he has any questions. Kenneth says, no, and that pretty much everything that was said was really spot-on about life, about everything. Sheri asks Kenneth if he was holding that guilt towards his mom and he said, "Yes, and for a lot of my family members. Before Debra even told me to picture myself next to God, I was already imagining Him standing there and I was looking into His eyes. I saw God. He was looking directly into my eyes." Kenneth then said he felt like he got the shivers all the way from his head to his toes. Kenneth felt God's pure love!!

⚜  ⚜  ⚜

After Kenneth's second healing session, he was back to perfect health and form. He was a completely different person. He began to connect with his family and mother again and reunited with old friends. He returned to work at his family's business. His entire life changed for the better very quickly, but he would soon find that some old habits die hard.

# CHAPTER TEN
# FIGHTING ADDICTION:
# GOD IS ON YOUR SIDE

## Kenneth's Third and Final Healing
## July 18, 2014

Seven months after Kenneth's healing at The Logos Center, he succumbed to his addiction and began to use heroin again. This time he quickly admitted fault and sought help. Kenneth has spent the last year battling his addiction. He now knows that he belongs to God, not himself. This clarity did not exist before his accident and healing.

On July 11, 2014, Kenneth's mother advised Sheri that Kenneth would be facing charges stemming from his heroin use. Jennifer requested another healing session for her son. God had once again brought Kenneth back so He could have His final words with him about his addiction.

The Healing Session
Kenneth lies on the healing table. Debra begins, "I feel it is very important to say these words. We are honored to have you here on our table because it is not easy for someone your age to come back here again and sit on this table. You are here because you have the trust. God is saying we are human, we get off track, we get off balance but that doesn't mean that God is upset with us. He just wants to get you back in line. The beautiful thing is that you know it and you showed up and you

are willing to receive it. That is a trust and a love that you have between yourself and God.

"Look, we are not all perfect and sometimes we do need a realignment or a readjustment. The first time you were here, you weren't really here because you were in a hospital. You were given a miracle and you made a choice that day. When you get off your path and away from your choice, God has to bring you back. He will have words with you about the choice you made."

Debra continues, "Before you even lay on this table, God was giving me words from the moment you stepped into this healing center. You stand tall and you stand strong. Kenneth, what that shows me is that you are still standing in God's light for you are standing in confidence. Those who don't carry that confidence can't stand strong. They kind of shrug their shoulders and they don't feel that strength. You have that strength still. You may not feel that strong, but you have it within you. What we are going to do today is listen. You will be balanced, realigned, and recentered with this energy. Your body is going to be worked on and we are going to go to a space where you are not in this room. Do not think about what is happening to your body. Don't think with your mind about what is happening, just leave it behind. Just follow my words.

"So as we center ourselves and get used to this energy, the two of us are going to take a walk while Sheri is anchoring us in this room and also sending healing energy to your body. The two of us are going to take a simple walk. You can imagine this in your mind as I am describing our journey. You have some pressures on your chest so we will also take those pressures off. We tune in to this energy. Remember that it is good to be vulnerable right now because you are in God's space. If tears come to your eyes, allow them and do not hold them in. This is your time. This is your direct connection. There is a part of me that feels a little angry. You are a little angry. I am going to express what I feel is inside you. Only God would know this."
At this point, God begins speaking directly to Kenneth.

"There is anger because you didn't know it was going to be so hard. 'If I can have a miracle, then why isn't everything else in my life going great? Why does everything else have to be so hard? I didn't ask for that. So I am angry because I made choices that I felt I had to do in order to survive. This may be the wrong choice but I did it not knowing that the consequences were so high.' I know you are upset, but it doesn't come easily because I am trying to get you to stand in my light. If everything were easy, Kenneth, you would push me aside. I want you to feel you need me. It got you back to needing me. But Kenneth, I don't want you to go to these deep, deep places to need me. I want you to need me and want me every day because I want you every day. When those times are really, really bad and you are angry, you ask, 'Why does life have to be so hard? Why do I have to do this?' You are angry and you never, ever turn to me. You may have said this to me, but you never trusted and asked me. You never trust and ask that I could bring it to you, that I would be your way.

"I am your way. I am your only way. I will bring you things that you have never had before. I will be the one to feed you. If I can give you the miracle, then I can bring everything else to you too. I will make it hard at times because it will make you who I want you to be. You will trust in me more because all you will have is me. Don't just call on me at the last minute. I want to be there through every step. Trust in me."

Debra continues, "It doesn't make sense right now, but it will. It is not like God is the one making you go through all this hardship. It doesn't have to be hard. You are facing it. God is saying that if you connected with Him through each phase, through each step, He would help you through each step and you wouldn't be where you are today. You would be somewhere else."

Debra feels Kenneth's internal wall go up when she delivers God's words to Kenneth. She says, "You don't need a lecture and your wall just went up and you are not going to listen.

God says, 'I am not trying to lecture you. I am trying to teach you. I am trying to hold you. I am trying to love you. I am trying to protect you. I am trying to give you everything you need. I am trying to show you. Some doors had to close and you didn't want them to and you fought to keep those doors open. When these doors are meant to be closed, it is going to be harder for you to go through them. And if you go through those doors, then you are going down the wrong path. You have to trust even if it's not what you want.'"

Debra feels Kenneth's wall go down again and says, "Thank you for opening up again just now. I want you to stay in this space. Do not look at those words as a lecture, please, because then you will tune this all out. Please look at it as a teaching out of love. God is telling you, 'I want to go back to our agreement. Remember the day that you stood with me? You remember looking down at your body and you told me you wanted to go back. Remember that day? Nothing was told how it was going to be when you came back, except that you would be whole again. You did make an agreement with me. I gave you the choice to come back. But I also gave you something else to take with you. It is a knowing in your heart and a knowing in your mind that with God all things are possible. And I am the only reason that you are here today. If you stand in that truth and you continue to remember, then that will lead you the right way. I gave you the biggest gift ever, Kenneth. I gave you life. I gave you life again. Life is a gift and you almost lost it. You are forgetting one thing. You are forgetting to honor me within you. In order for you to have life again, you had this new mission and this new voice to show that I exist. I gave you a miracle, a miracle of life. Life can come crashing down and be taken away very easily if you choose not to stand in it, this agreement I chose for you. Go back to that day and remember that date. Look at the date and do not forget it. You said you wanted it. You need to honor it.'

"You remember looking down and you remember seeing your body and you had a split second to make a choice because in that split second, you could've been gone. And what you have that is such a gift, you would no longer have. I want you to look at your surroundings. When I say surroundings, it means the people who love you. All you have to do, Kenneth, here on Earth is to love yourself by doing what is right and by loving God and loving those around you. Everything else will fall into place. As God stands here, I want you to speak to Him in your mind. I heard you say, 'I am sorry.' God says there is no need to be sorry. You are learning and this is your lesson. It is making you who you need to be. It is okay, but no more. No more mistakes. It is like Dorothy and the yellow brick road; she followed the yellow brick road. You have to follow the white line. Follow God's walk. Follow His bright light. The only way you are going to follow that path is by connecting with Him. He will lead the way.

"God is hugging you and saying it is going to be okay. It is going to be okay. You don't have to hold it all in. You don't have to act all strong. He is holding you and He will make sure everything is okay. But God is telling you that you have to do your part, Kenneth: 'I am asking you to do your part with me. Just stand in my light. Call on me for every need. Talk to me when you are angry. Talk to me when you are mad. Talk to me when you are sad. Talk to me when you are happy. I am your best friend. I am your everything. I want to know it all. I want to be there for it all. Don't feel you are alone. I am holding you. I am loving you.'

"God says, 'My hand is always open and my heart is always here. I am always there in any time of need, but you have to ask and you have to talk to me. If you are just assuming I am going to do things without you talking to me, then you will never know it came from me. It doesn't work that way. You have to have the connection. You have to do the talk to do the walk. I hold you today, Kenneth, in my light. I am going to put protection around you. I want you to know that the next steps are to make you strong. I am going to shield you in my light and my protection and I want you to know that no matter what happens, I have you.

"'You are going to be my voice. You are going to show the power that I gave you and you are just growing into it. It is okay because it takes time and you are young. I don't expect anybody who is young to miraculously be the perfect one, but I am molding you to be my perfect one. I need you to be strong and I need you to be confident and I need you to be able to stand in my light. I need you to say it is not easy, but with God all things are possible. I want you to say, I am only human and we all make mistakes and God has shown me that through our mistakes, He forgives. He says these are lessons for us to become who we are because we are not perfect.'"

Debra continues, "Remember that God was never once hurtful to you and He saw everything you did. All He did was love you. That is what we say to others who want to judge: Why do you judge so harshly when God doesn't judge at all? I am proud of you, Kenneth, for being you and for making this choice. Remember this day, as it is very profound, for it is a gift. It is a gift of knowledge that you didn't have before. But it took you to go through what you did to receive it. So it is a blessing. You wouldn't say what you did was a blessing, but it is because it could have been so much worse. Now you know how not to get to those places anymore. Trust that God will make it all okay. It frees you from worry. It frees you because it will show you that it will all be there for you. Trust and you will receive all that you need.

"This is a blessing that this day has happened because God is able to teach. God is your teacher. There is no better teacher. With that, you come back and God is still looking down at you. He is not leaving. He has never left. You left Him, remember that.

"Thank you, Kenneth, for being here. Thank you for being you. I am proud of you and I love you. There are consequences to all of our actions, but God can have His hand in on it too, watch and see. With that, I want you to know that God has left. Do not forget the words that I have said to you from God. They could not be repeated if I tried. Know that your entire body was infused with His light and love and energy, giving you the strength to get you through what you need to get through. Your face and your story are going to be known. Honor this day by giving thanks to God." With Debra's closing words, Sheri places a seal of God's love around Kenneth.

Once Kenneth's healing session is complete, it is his mother's turn. Jennifer enters the room and lies on the table. Debra begins, "Jennifer, as you are on this healing table, I want you to know that because of your faith, everything that has happened was the answer to your prayers. Your son made a choice that day. He could've left in a split second but he chose not to. And because he chose not to, you need to trust that a miracle happened that day. You need to trust that he has a mission and a duty but he is just learning. He is learning how to accept God every day. If he didn't go through these hardships, he wouldn't learn. In his session, God told him, 'I am not mad at you. I am teaching you. Just because we are given life does not mean that it is going to be easy. You need me every step of the way.'

"He is learning. Look at what is happening as a blessing and not as a hardship. He is being molded into the person he is supposed to be. Without this lesson and without this hardship, these words that were given to him would have no meaning today. If God can shield and heal your son in a miracle, then you need to trust that everything else is going to work out the way God wants it to work out. Trust it because it is going to make him who he needs to be.

"Your son is young and I want you to think of a wall with many hooks on it. On these hooks are many hats and your son doesn't know which hat to wear. He is learning. Should I put this hat on today? Well, maybe if I put this hat on, life will be a little easier. Or should I grab that hat? Which hat is going to best fit me? Who am I? He has learned today that he doesn't need a hat. All he needs is God. He also was told that the only thing in life that is important is love. He is learning and God does not judge him. God is protecting him. He is proud for this day because if he did not go through what he went through, he wouldn't be here. He wouldn't have learned the lesson. He needed this to learn who he is supposed to be. He received a gift of knowledge, a gift of strength, a gift of courage, and so did you today. You didn't know that there was a blessing behind it all. It frees you and makes you feel like you don't have so much pressure and worry in your heart.

"God is in control and He is molding your son into who he needs to be today. Whatever happens, I trust. Remember that God has His hand in on this just like He did when He performed the miracle. He hears all of your prayers. It will be what it needs to be. Thy will be done the way it needs to be done. You may not understand it, but we will trust it. It will free you, knowing that it was God's way. Let the control go. Either way, you win. Either outcome, you win. Why, because it is God's outcome. He is molding Kenneth in His light. It frees you from the worry and the burden that you have taken on. Take a deep breath in and feel all the worries just leave you. You feel lighter and you can breathe again. It is lifted and has been taken from you."

Sheri gives Jennifer energy during the time Debra has been speaking and also releases Jennifer's worries and gives them to God. Debra continues, "You can smile now. You deserve to be happy. We take the pain away and we breathe in love and light, freeing us from all this worry and this burden. When we walk out of here, we feel less worried and less stressed. A mother's job is never done, but this will free you if you let his Father in heaven be the one in control. Remember that all this stress is to your body like bad oil is to a car. We need to decompress. We need to step away. We need to do what is right for you. Smile and take a moment to be happy. Do what pleases you because you deserve to be happy. It is going to feed your soul and that is what you need to be happy. Don't feel guilty for doing it. We give thanks for your bringing your son in. We give thanks for you being on this table and surrounding your son with this gift and blessing that we received today."

Jennifer's healing is now complete. She cries tears of relief and joy. She feels that a burden has just been lifted from her.

# Chapter Eleven
## Surviving Cancer: The Gift of Living, The Gift of Hope

**Denise Meek Healing Session**
**September 30, 2012**

Denise Meek (center) with Debra Martin & Sheri Getten

Denise Meek attended a free healing session on Sunday, September 30, 2012, at The Logos Center in Scottsdale, Arizona. At least one hundred people waited in line for a ten-minute healing session. There were so many people that it would be impossible for Debra and Sheri to see everyone in one day. Of all the people in attendance, though, there was no doubt that Denise was divinely chosen to have a healing that day.

Debra and Sheri were told nothing about each person who entered the Threshold Room. During Denise's session, God came through showing her cancer. At that time she was told God would stop her cancer from spreading but this could not be healed in a ten-minute session. After the session, she started crying. Denise thought she was just coming in to receive a message from her dad. She never felt her cancer would be touched upon. She was amazed at how precisely, accurately, and quickly all the details of her cancer were revealed in her ten-minute session.

Denise returned for a private session the following week. During this session, ten spiritual surgeons were present and performed a delicate surgery. God said through Debra that this surgery could not have been performed in the physical form. This was the only healing session Debra and Sheri didn't record, so below is Denise's narrative in her own words.

## My Journey to Debra and Sheri and the Story of My Miracles

I am amazed at the path my life took to get to this place. It truly makes me believe in the divine power of God.

I can't remember exactly when I was officially diagnosed with cancer. Though it was late summer of 2011, the date isn't clear because I had three biopsies with different results. The doctors needed to confirm which kind of lung cancer I had. Of course I got the bad one: small cell lung cancer. It spreads rapidly to other organs in the body and especially likes to take over the brain and the bones, which is exactly what happened in my case. After everything else I'd been through in life, it didn't seem quite fair that this would be the cause of my demise. I fell into a deep depression, waking every day to the thought that it was going to be my last. I never smiled and I lived in fear every second of every day. Though I was going through the motions, I wasn't *feeling* anything because I was so scared of not knowing what was coming next.

I started to think about Debra for some unknown reason. Six years ago I had had a reading over the phone with her but I couldn't shake the feeling that I was being pushed in her direction, that I needed to contact her. I found her website and contacted her for a reading. On September 30, 2012, approximately one year after the cancer diagnosis, my friend and I decided to attend the healing session at The Logos Center with Debra and Sheri. They were speaking in front of a large group and had offered to do ten-minute healing sessions on those who wanted to experience a healing session in the Threshold Room. I was skeptical that anything could be done for me, but Debra had given me a very accurate reading back in 2006, so I decided to take the chance. What was the worst that could happen?

I was hoping for my dad and great-grandmother to come through to give me comfort, so I could deal with my small cell lung cancer diagnosis and everything to come. The oncologist had told me that *if* I made it through the first year, I would still only have a ten percent chance of living three years. I specifically had not told Debra the reason why I was there. I guess I was kind of testing her abilities (and spirit) to see if she really could help me.

I stepped into the Threshold Room and lay on the healing table. The room was darkened and Debra was under the table, out of my sight. Sheri began connecting me with the energy fields. It took less than two minutes for Debra to tell me she felt pain in the right lung area and said she saw cancer. She got it immediately! Through my tears, I told her I did in fact have cancer. I told them it had spread to my brain already and that this type of cancer spreads to other organs quickly. They both started working on the healing, Debra speaking from

God and Sheri bringing the healing energy to my body. They told me it would take more than this ten-minute session to complete the healing. Debra told me God said He would keep the cancer from spreading to any other areas. They suggested that I come back for an individual private healing session for the work to be completed, so I definitely agreed to come back.

The second session was on October 4, 2012. I was excited yet nervous at the same time. There was so much emotion from me and so much energy from Sheri and so much insight from Debra that I can't begin to describe it. During the session God gave me the choice to remain on Earth and be given another chance or to let go because my set time had expired. I chose to stay here on Earth and signed a new life contract with God.

Then the real work began as ten spiritual surgeons were asked to perform their miracles. At one point Debra saw them remove a small mass (she said it looked like a small ball) that was near my heart area. I told her after the healing that my doctors had already biopsied a mass in that area to determine if it was cancer.

When the healing was finished, I went home feeling very drained of energy, yet very peaceful. I cried for hours, releasing all the fear I had been holding on to for the past year. It was cathartic because for the first time in over a year, I wasn't thinking about dying. The healing released all the fears that had consumed me since my diagnosis. When you are given three years to live, it makes you see everything with a sense of finality. On this day I began living again. I had faith in what Debra and Sheri told me. The biopsy that had been done before the healing— in the area near my heart exactly where Debra saw the surgeons work—had come back negative for cancer but had shown on a scan that cancer was likely to develop. Less than a month after my healing session, I received the news that my PET scan and brain MRI were clear! There was no sign of the cancer and the mass that they biopsied had completely disappeared. It was GONE! I was CANCER FREE!

I truly and firmly believe this was a direct result of Debra's ability to see, hear, and know what needed to be healed and Sheri's abilities of receiving the healing energy and knowing where to place it. They are messengers of God. I don't spend my days worrying any longer because of the work they did. I received a gift: the gift of living. The gift of hope. I live my life differently as a more forgiving, patient, and loving person. I try to see the beauty and good everywhere I look. By no means am I the most cheerful person you will ever meet, but I can give my bad attitude a rest and see things more positively. In the end, I figured out, that's all we can do.

My journey to Debra and Sheri took six long years of my own disasters, but it was worth it to be brought to God in this way. My last two checkup scans in June 2013 have shown that I am still cancer free since my healing.

⚜ ⚜ ⚜

Denise went from having a ten percent chance of survival to being cancer free. This healing was a true miracle.

Denise contacted Debra and Sheri via email on August 24, 2013, to let them know the great news. She also shared that she was having trouble with her balance. She had been walking funny and was unable to drive. Debra knew right away that Denise needed to come in for a second healing so that this time God's words would be recorded. An appointment was made. God would have His conversation with Denise.

# Chapter Twelve
# God Speaks to Denise

### Denise Meek Final Healing Session
### August 29, 2013

Denise is positioned on the healing table. Debra begins, "At this time I want you to relax. I want you to know you are safe. I want to note that this is your third time on this table. The first time was a ten-minute session. The second time was your major healing, which was not recorded. And this time we are recording so that you remember the words that come through and that God can say what it is that He needs to voice today. It is time now for me to go under the table and become one with you.

"The minute you walked in the door, I became dizzy and I can feel it on the right part of my head/brain. It is almost in the temple area and then right in the front. If you look into the eyes and go straight up, it is in there. And I get this dizzy feeling at times where I become very nauseous. I am feeling pain now in the back right, upper part of my head. I would say back right corner. I am getting pain right there and they are definitely showing me there is something right there." Debra cries out from pain.

"I was just administered medicine and I can taste it through my nose, which means there is going to be some kind of surgery done to this area of your brain." Debra tells Denise to relax her eyes because everything is connected to her eyes, especially the right one. "What I am seeing is all of the veins and the little things that all attach to the back of your eye. You are just going to relax and receive. I feel like there is a lot of pressure coming in to this back part of the head, it is almost as if a drill or something is going in right through the top back part of the head. I can see that there is a long scope that is going to go in where they just went in with the drill. It is microscopic going in, very tiny, very long. It is interesting because they are making me put my knees up and I have to hold them very tight. So I have my arms around my knees just holding them and my body in this tight position."

Debra lets out a scream of pain and begins breathing deeply. "They are going through my head. I feel a little tube that I envision like a straw. And this straw is like a vacuum tube and it is plastic and it is cream-colored and it is not see-through.. They are going to vacuum out all that doesn't need to be in there." At the same time, Sheri feels magnets of energy going through her hands to Denise's head. Debra continues, "Picture a brain that has a white mass that looks like glue on the side. You're thinking, *How am I going to get that out of all the crevasses?* You would think you could not remove it, but God can.

"They are explaining everything so specifically so you can understand how intense and how delicate the surgery is and that this really couldn't be performed by anyone else but God. The mass is like glue that ran into all these other places and it stuck and there is not anything else they could do to take it out. But God has His special ways so we are just going to let Him take this out."

Sheri comments that the energy over her head is incredibly strong and palpable. It is like a magnetic force all around her head.

Debra explains to Denise how the spiritual surgeons are using a vacuum that is removing the mass from her brain and releasing it to God. Sheri's task is to use her energy to melt and release the mass so that the surgeons can use the tube to extract it and bring it to the surface and suck it out. They work together; the surgery could not be performed without help from both sides.

Then she announces that God has words for Denise. Debra takes a deep breath and begins. "Put your hands out and interlock them. The reason you are feeling this firm, tight grip is because God is saying, 'Those are my hands holding your hand tightly and we have been on this journey together. I am holding your hand.' And even if you try to let it go right now, you can't because God is holding your hands and He is saying, 'You stepped in to every part of this healing, every part. You have done your job, your mission. Now it is like you asked and you received and I gave you everything, healed completely, gone. Remember I am still holding your hands and holding them tightly. Do not be afraid now to walk forward. You are thinking, *Now what do I do, now where do I go?* It is hard to breathe and it is hard to know. It is not up to you to decide or make the decisions. If you let the worry go, I will hold your hand and guide you to what you need to do. The doors will open. Do not be afraid to walk, knowing I have got your hand. I am one step ahead of you. I see everything and you just need to follow me.'"

Debra continues, "And it is not always easy just because you are holding God's hand and He is saying to follow Him. Well, where are we going? It is your job to search the avenues, to open the doors. But God will place the ones that are really supposed to be open in front of you and you will know because they will come out of nowhere.

"I want you to put your arms out now and put your palms up and I want to scan your entire body. Sheri will place her energy on your entire body from your head to your toes." Sheri feels tremendous energy moving through her to Denise. Debra says she feels like her skin is going to fall off because her hands are so hot and she says that she normally does not feel this kind of heat. It is so intense that she grabs Sheri's ankles, doubling the energy going into Denise.

Debra says, "I feel like I just became numb, I feel like I am not here." Debra says there is so much going on right now that if she even tries to move or get up, she can't. The third eye is being opened up too on Denise so that she can see more clearly now too. Debra then says, "The energy in my hands is burning me. It just shows me that I know, because I don't ever get this feeling of burning energy and I am being shown and I feel how much energy is going through Denise right now. It is so intense that it hurts and it is going through the tops of the palms of your hands, and I am not sure if the palms of your hands hurt or if I am just feeling it.

"You have played a big role in this healing, Denise. You have done everything that I have asked you to do. So don't question this next process. Know that thy will be done. What we are healing, thy will be done. Everything has a process. Everything has steps and layers. We did the first ten-minute healing session to stop your cancer from spreading. Then we did the second healing and we took it all out and your cancer was healed. This was a true miracle. Then your body needed to settle into that new state. And now we are fine-tuning it."

Debra says she feels like she is going to cry. She has tears in her eyes as she speaks more words from God: "I worked through you so you can be my divine angel here on Earth to speak the power that not only lies within you, but that comes from me. And when others can connect to it one on one in the way that you have, look at the power that you can create. When I say create, it means my creation, my divine connection, all lies within. I hear your prayers; I hear them and I have answered every single one of them. You have stepped into every process, so know this is about divine timing. Allow the process to take form. You are my MIRACLE!"

Debra pauses as more medicine is administered, and she says she feels it in her nose. She continues, "God is showing me that you signed a contract with Him. 'I have done every-thing for you and answered every prayer and have made you ᴜᴜs divine angel here on Earth. You signed a contract. But Denise, you are forgetting that I signed it too. I won't let you down. You have not come this far to fail now. Your mission has just begun. Connect with me. I am in you. You have a purpose and a mission now. Your final step has been done. It is complete. Your mission has just begun and I am infusing you and I am giving you the keys to hold. It is as if you are getting a new car and it is up to you to put the keys in and start the ignition and drive it to wherever you are supposed to go. You hold the key. Connect with me. I am in you. You are the driver of your own vehicle, your body.

"'You can have the impossible. Reach, for it is here for you to have and to hold. This is bigger than what you know, Denise, for when you start speaking, for those who listen, you have proof, and you have living proof. You went through it. You felt it and you healed it, you became one with it, you let go of the fear. You did it all and you did it with me and that's why you signed the contract. I am not going to let you down.

"'So remember, please put those hands back together and know that I am holding your hands every step of the way. If you choose to shut my door and not hold my hand, that is your choice and your outcome becomes different. If you stand in my light, I am the way, I am the truth, and I will guide you and I will hold your hand from here to eternity.'"

Debra reveals that Denise's loved ones from the other side have entered the room. "I have someone special here for you. You have wanted to connect with him since the day you came in to this room. Your grandmother, your father—they're here. Your father smiles because he is so very proud of you."

Debra feels a headache coming on and says the spiritual surgeons are finishing up in this area of the head. Debra smells smoke and asks if Denise or her family members ever smoked. Denise confirms that both she and her father used to smoke. Debra tells Denise, "You need to stay away from anybody who smokes, even if it means you have to leave a restaurant or a grocery store or wherever. Stay away from cig-arette smoke and walk the opposite direction because right now you are so pure that you need to just stay away."

Debra says, "Now, if you all of a sudden just smell smoke, you will know that it is just your dad in the room. Your dad has a sense of humor and says, 'If we want to smoke up here, it is not going to kill us.' They are watching you, they are loving you, and they are protecting you. Don't think that anything you say to them is not heard, because it is. And your dad heard you say, 'I just wish that someone was here taking care of me.' You have always had to be the strong one. He is saying what you've gone through has made you the person you are today and it all has worked out the way it was supposed to.

"You have been granted angel wings today. So if people look at you differently, it is because they see the angel that is inside. You carry a lot of power; use it."

Debra announces that the surgeons have removed the tubes from Denise's body. Sheri continues to place energy into Denise to complete the healing. She marvels at the amount of energy that is still going in through the top of Denise's head. The energy spreads from the crown of Denise's head all the way down to her toes. Sheri's hands hurt from the intensity. Debra says to Denise, "Your body went through a lot today. Just let everything settle. Your healing will continue to work as you go home and go to sleep.

"The three of us have gone through a lot on this journey. Cancer of the brain and lung and that mass, and now a clean bill of health. You wonder, *Why did this all happen?* God wanted this shown. You have the proof.

"So here you are now, just fine-tuning and getting to hear the words that God wanted you to hear today. It just makes everything else from the beginning until now complete. And Denise, I am in awe of listening to God speak to you. The strength, the courage that you have shown to overcome all of the fear that could've destroyed you and you didn't allow it.

Both Sheri and I are in awe of not only your faith, but also your trust and your connection with God to make it happen. You are a miracle. And God said, 'You are my miracle.' That was powerful. I can now hear the words 'Rejoice, rejoice, rejoice.'

"The first time we saw you, there was so much fear. You were told by doctors that you weren't going to survive and the unknown was frightening. And oh my, you have to think every day, *When am I going to die?* You reversed it, you stopped thinking that way, and you listened to the words God gave you. You became one with Him. You released the fear and you allowed the healing to take place by stepping into it. We are so proud of you."

Denise says, "I needed you two also."

Debra says, "Three in one, we did it together. We are always here for you, Denise, we love you."

Denise says through her tears, "I love you too."

Sheri fills Denise with God's white light and love. Sheri then says, "We now give thanks to God for this healing. We give thanks to Denise for stepping into this healing. We give thanks to God for using Debra and me as His instruments." Debra hears hallelujahs being sung and says, "We now complete this healing with the three of us saying the Lord's Prayer."

# Chapter Thirteen
# God's Words for Anyone
# Facing Cancer

## Katy Jones Healing Session
## October 5, 2013

This chapter is excerpted from a recorded healing session for a woman we will call Katy Jones (she requested that her real name not be used) who was diagnosed with cancer. Debra and Sheri feel these words will help anyone who has cancer.

The Healing Session

Debra cries out in pain and says, "There is something in my foot, the bottom of my foot. You are afraid to walk through this, you are really scared about this and it is almost like there is a thorn in your foot. You are almost paralyzed. You think, *How am I going to do this? How am I going to walk like this?* Your mind is taking over the heart and what you need to do is release the mind. Don't worry, don't think, because you have to let this all come from your heart and you have to walk through this with the love of God and nothing else.

"And He will walk through this with you and He will hold your hand every step of the way. You have asked Him and He is here. He will hold your hand. Allow Him to walk the walk with you. Don't be afraid to walk it because there are such grander things on the other side. Things can be tough, but the outcome is glorious. Nothing is easy."

Debra says, "Oh goodness, oh goodness, oh goodness," as she receives more medicine from the spiritual surgeons. "So what they are doing is preparing your body for what you are about to go through with your doctors. So that is what we are seeing right now. We are going to all of the areas to prepare you."

Debra's foot pain continues. She tells Katy, "What I want you to do right now is listen to this, as these are words from God. When I speak right now, I want you to know that these are not my words, these are God's words. Anytime I am speaking to you, this is not coming from my mind, this is coming from God. This is what God has to share with you: 'When you sit in the chair to have your medicine administered, pay attention to your free arm. Put your palm up and relax it. Know that I am here holding your hand through this entire process and I will be standing next to you in that room holding your hand. Even if someone else is there holding your hand, know that I am too.

"'So as I hold your hand, I want you to know that I am watching the medicine that goes through your body. The doctors may be administering it, but I am the one altering it. I am going to alter it to what it needs to be for your body. Everything that goes in is what I am overseeing. You do not need to fear it, but take it in, knowing it is I and it is my medicine that the doctors are administering to you through your veins, through your organs, through your cells. This is coming from me and as I hold your hand, know that you can smile and accept this gift that I am administering through you.

"'When you put your hand up and you allow me to hold it, you may close your eyes, you may see me standing there, you may feel my presence, you may feel calm. And you may just have this smile on your face, knowing that I am the one overseeing it and with that you have nothing to fear. Just let me hold your hand.'" Debra's voice changes; instead of the powerful voice that conveyed God's words, it becomes very calm and soft. "As God stands in this room holding your hand right now, I want you to feel how this room has shifted into this peace and how you just feel so calm. It's like you are not part of your body. It's like you can feel and know your body is lying on the table, but all of a sudden I don't feel anything from my body. I feel numb.

"That is because you are connecting your spirit with God. Know that it is only your body that is going to go through changes; do not allow your spirit to change. As your body gets weaker, hold my hand and allow your spirit to get stronger because the two of us being strong will give you the energy your body needs to heal. God is telling you, 'I want you to know that I have touched everything that needs to be healed. If I did not say it, it does not mean that it was not touched. What's happening is my white light is going from the top of your head and it is spinning through you like a tornado. That's my love, that's my healing going inside and empowering you and giving you the strength to walk through this process with me. Give me your worries, give me your fears, and surrender them for they do you no good. They just slow down the process.'"

Debra's voice again becomes soft and emotional as she says, "God is still standing at the left side of this table. He has one hand in your palm and the other one around your arm. He is looking into your eyes. If you need a vision of this, look to the right and look at the picture of Jesus hanging on the wall. Focus on His eyes right now, connect with the eyes."

Katy says, "I see this," and has tears in her eyes.

Both Katy and Sheri are crying. Debra says, "Connect and feel Him, He is here."

Katy says, "It is so beautiful."

Debra says, "Yes, and it makes you feel numb inside."

Katy says, "It feels so good and it is soothing," as she looks at the picture of Jesus.

Then Debra speaks again. "It is this overwhelming feeling of love that you can't describe, and what I am trying to tell you is that this numbness is good. It is weightless, it is emotionless, it is just pure."

Katy says, "Yes."

Debra continues, "It feels like you're not here but you are in this place with this amount of love that you cannot explain, and He is infusing you right now with His love. Look in His eyes and stay focused, stay focused." All three women are crying because of the amount of love they are feeling in the room. Then God speaks through Debra. "Remember my eyes, whatever you have to do. I want you to close your eyes right now and remember these eyes. That is what you are going to focus on anytime you have worry and anytime you do healing. Remember that every time you take in your medicine from doctors, I am infusing you with another healing, standing at your side like I am right now, looking at you.

"I am infusing you with this vision of who I am so you can take me with you through this process. That's what you are to do. I am infusing this inside of you, and you are allowing it by looking in my eyes and remembering this feeling at each and every one of your sessions with the doctors as well.

"I am speaking to you right now. Connect with my eyes and look at me because I am speaking to you as a father is speaking to his child. You need to look into my eyes when I speak to you as a sign of respect, a sign of honor, as if I am the only one in this room. I am speaking to you right now. This does not just happen; this took time to evolve. This didn't all come overnight. What happened is you started walking in this life, feeling that you were unworthy. And I am looking at you and you are my child and you are worthy of it all. Every one of my children deserves to feel worthy. Others beat you up emotionally, took you down, depleted you of your self-worth. I am here to put you on that highest pedestal because you are worth it all. You need to know you are worthy because I am standing here for you now. Your dignity, your self-worth, who you are is who I created and shame, shame, shame on anyone on this Earth who shatters another one of my children's souls.

"I am here to take that pain away, to allow you to become the person I created. You will have more strength and more power than you've ever had before. I want you to envision this next step because these words will hold value for you if I show them to you in my eyes. You are going to stand next to me. And you are looking down on your daughter lying on this table. And I want you to imagine that she has what you have, and she is experiencing what you are experiencing. And when you look down on her you say, 'You are my child and I love you unconditionally and you are worthy of it all.' Now do you understand what I am saying to you?"

Katy says, "I am worthy, I am loved. But why is it so hard to love ourselves?"

Through Debra, God replies, "Imagine yourself as my child. You're standing next to me, looking at your body lying on the table. It is your body that I created. Your spirit is outside the body, standing next to me looking at your shell (body) on the table. Look at the amazing, intricate machine that is you. You have eyes to see. You have a tongue to taste and speak. You have ears to hear. You have a heart to feel, to love. Your heart is how you give your own daughter unconditional love. Your heart is how you feel my unconditional love for you. It is the brain that does not allow your heart to feel that you are worthy to love yourself. But I love you, my child. Know this and trust this. I love you, and you need to love yourself.

"When you love yourself, you know you are worthy of receiving this healing. Love encompasses all. Love is a powerful, powerful energy and it is the only thing we take with us when we die. I am giving you my love and showing you that if I love you, then you need to love yourself."

Katy says, "I love myself, I love myself."

"Beautiful, that is exactly what I want you to keep saying," Debra says. "I just felt more medicine go through my nose. Just sit quietly and allow these areas that God has touched to be infused with His white light. Like I said, we had this white light like a tornado go from the top of your head. I want it to infuse your entire body, your organs, your cells, everything from the top of your head to the bottom of your toes, inside and out. Please know that you are not alone and He is walking with you. And He is one step ahead of you every step of the way. Anytime that you feel that it is too hard for you to take that step, ask God. 'God, give me the strength, help me get out of bed, help me take that step. Help me to remove my fear. I surrender it to you each and every day.'

"Do not forget that He is standing through every chemotherapy session with you starting today. Do not forget that He sealed and put a lining on everything in your body so nothing else could be harmed. So this medicine that is being administered to your body is going to go only to the areas of your body that need to be destroyed and you don't have to worry about the other things that could happen.

"As doctors administer medicine in the hospital, God will alter anything that needs to be altered so that you are receiving only what your body needs. It is a good thing to say the following: 'Dear God, when taking these medicines, only allow my body to receive what it needs and please take out what it doesn't need.' This will go hand in hand with the rest of this process."

"Even though you may be having a difficult time right now, God hears you. He feels your pain and will come to you. Light your candle within. God is within each of us. Go within and have a direct connect with Him." - Debra and Sheri

# CHAPTER FOURTEEN
# CONFRONTING FEAR OF THE
# UNKNOWN

### Annette Puleo Healing Session
### April 6, 2014

Annette, far left, standing next to her two daughters, Lisa and Lana, and granddaughter Giovanna.

Annette grew up in the Bronx, New York. She met her husband at sixteen and was married at twenty-one. They had their first daughter, Marie-Elena, three and a half years later, and their second daughter, Lisa, eight years after their first. She then stayed home to raise her family and started babysitting when her girls got older. Soon after, she started teaching religious education through their parish and stayed on for fourteen years.

Annette's daughter Lisa contacted Debra and Sheri for a healing session. Lisa was desperate to help her mother because Annette had multiple health issues and it seemed as if she received more bad news from her doctors every day. Lisa also told Debra and Sheri that recently the doctor had found a mass in Annette's rectum. She told them that a sonogram and needle biopsy were scheduled for the next week to find out what kind of mass it was. Annette was not completely sold on the idea of a healing, though, and was visibly nervous when she and Lisa arrived at The Logos Center.

The Healing Session

Debra begins, "Annette, your job is to lie on this table and receive. So relax and let this session start." Debra goes under the table to become one with Annette and begins the healing session.

Debra says, "As I was standing at the foot of the healing table, I had a little headache, like a piercing pain in my head on the right side and I can feel it now. I can also feel it going down into my neck as if my neck hurts. I feel a little tension there. There are several things that can be happening right now—there is a lot on your shoulders and you carry a lot in your neck. I can feel it radiating down my neck on the right. I have to keep my neck kind of turned.

"Remember, we are scanning your entire body; we want to fine-tune everything from your head to your toes. So there may be things mentioned that you're not even aware of. The neck issues are happening because you carry a lot of the pressure in your neck. I just tasted some medicine." Debra coughs.

"I feel like they are rewiring, reconfiguring your brain. It's like your brain is a radio and they have to make sure that it stays on the right frequency so that when they realign, recenter, renew, and rebalance and take out whatever is causing you issues, this does not go back to the old. They are holding it, it's like holding an antenna in place but not tightening it, not sealing it, until the rest is aligned and done. So they are going to continue to hold this as we work down the body.

"Over to the right lower abdomen, I feel a gentle touch in the area of what was taken out or what was once worked on by doctors here in the physical. They gently touch this, making sure there is not scar tissue and making sure everything inside will flow and work properly. And when I push on that–oh, I just received more medicine–up above my belly button I can feel some pressure. We have a white light being pushed into the belly button but I feel tons of pressure in my upper abdomen. If we were going to go to your belly button and go four inches up, that's where we are starting. I don't know the body parts well enough to know what is right inside there but I do know that they are pointing to that center and I see a white light swirling in that area. I can feel my stomach starting to bloat. I can feel movement."

Debra cries out in pain. "It is being pumped, filled with water, liquids, and medicine. I can feel it bubbling inside. This whole area is starting to move. They are still working on the head and the neck. Oh, here we go–ugh!" Debra screams from the pain. "Okay, now that we bloated up the entire inside of your abdomen cavity, I am experiencing pain in my lower extremities. It is all the way across from the right to the left. Meanwhile my head is hurting in that one area so I will keep it straight and turned to the side."

Debra is breathing hard and has a hard time speaking. "They just went in with an instrument. They cut in right there. Oh my! I felt the prick. Ugh, ugh, so we have an instrument that is going in." Debra struggles to get through the pain.

Gasping, she says she doesn't know what is happening just feels the pain. "They went right into something! They took the instrument right into an area that is causing you the issues. They went right into it. They punctured it."

Debra takes several deep breaths, then continues, "I feel coolness that just came into the room. I can feel this coolness touch the outside perimeters of my body so that I know and feel this shift in the room. What I want you to do, Annette, is I want you to look over to the right where there is a picture of Jesus on this wall. I want you to look into the eyes of Jesus right now as He stands here. If you put your right palm up, I want you to feel that God is holding it. And as you look through His eyes, I want you to listen to these words, for these are God's words that He says to you. I feel like crying because I feel the presence, it is very strong. God says, 'I love you, I love you, you are a product of me, you carry me inside of you, you believe in me, and I believe in you. So as my teams, my workers, have these instruments in you and I hold your hand, you will say this in your mind, Annette.'"

Debra continues, "This is what God wants you to say while you look into His eyes: 'I no longer want this, I no longer deserve this, I no longer need this. God, I ask you to take this away. Please take this away here and now.' As God holds your hand He says, 'You deserve to be healed because you are a product of me and I love you.' So you can close your eyes and continue to know that He is holding your hand as we take out what is not needed." Debra struggles to breathe through the intense pain she feels.

"It's like they are piercing it, burning it, and they are cauterizing it, dissolving it; it will no longer hold anything that you do not deserve. I felt it being taken out." Debra feels a rash coming on all over her belly. She tells Annette that she must be allergic to certain medicines. "I feel very itchy. So the medicines that they used I am going to have to change. Now my lower abdomen is very tender, especially where they put the tubes in, and I want you to know that when we take something out we have to put something in. What we are putting in and filling you up with is beautiful white light. You can almost feel like your stomach is becoming bloated and feeling full. It's because the white light is going in there and it is sealing it with God's love and light and healing, and we are infusing this whole area.

"Now this will become tender, your entire abdomen cavity, and when it happens you may become tired. You should sleep pretty well tonight. You were administered a lot of medicine. Just like a real surgery you would have to go home and rest. You have to honor your body and allow this to work through you. So as we continue to place the white light inside you, we are looking at the rest of the body to make sure you're aligned and centered, to make sure that everything is going to flow in unison and harmoniously with your body. Remember, we were at the head and they were rewiring your brain knowing that we want to think differently. 'I no longer have this, I no longer own this, and this is no longer a part of me. I gave this to God.' So if you feel sick or worried, all you have to say is, 'God, I know you healed me, I know this is just part of my healing process.' Sometimes we won't feel anything but if you do, you need to place it in God's hands and say, 'I know you healed this, it's no longer a part of me.'"

Debra starts to breathe heavily again. "I am receiving a little more medicine; I have to put my legs up in the air for some reason." She pulls her knees up to her chest. "Okay," Debra says through deep breaths. "We usually see light go through the top of the head. I am also going to place it in through your private parts, your woman parts, it's going through this area. I see white light like a scope going in. As this scope goes in, it shoots out God's light, infusing you, radiating all the areas that need His touch.

"I can feel some pressure in my right ear while they are working on this lower area. They are opening up your ear so that you are in tune with the spirit world, meaning you're able to think more clearly, hear more clearly, and with the hearing you have a knowing and a trusting that becomes stronger. Your connection with God is stronger. Your intuition is your line to Him. But it comes through your hearing, through your mind, through your ears.

"My feet feel a little swollen. When I move my toes they feel swollen. So you are retaining water. So what we want to do is make sure the energy is flowing up and around and through all your veins so that you don't retain too much. Drink lots of water, so that you can let out what you don't need. As the light is inside you, it is radiating, I feel it pulsating but I can also feel it pinching in the area that they went in with the instruments. It's interesting how I feel like this white light is a tube and it is radiating everything down there. It's igniting everything as it pushes its way up, making sure that it is touching everything that needs to be touched.

"Imagine gold shimmer as if it were glitter, but gold like angel dust. I want you to see it coming down, and as this shimmering goes inside you, I am now seeing it as more white than gold. This shimmer of white is actually going to an area where you had prior surgery, healing what was worked on. This shimmering white is going through all your cells; I feel like they are going into your atoms. The shimmering is activating all the good cells, boosting your immune system. We want to make sure that there are no bad cells. We are going to use this white shimmering light throughout your entire body."

Debra takes more deep breaths. "I feel pressure in my temples, and I feel like I have to shake my body. It's like a salad dressing bottle when all the good stuff is at the bottom. We need to shake your body, Annette, and loosen up all the stuff you don't need and replace it with all this good throughout.

"So now I am rocking"–Debra is rocking on her back under the table with her knees up to her chest—"and as I am shaking, it hurts my abdomen. There are parts that have been worked on that I haven't even mentioned. I only mention the places that I feel, but I want you to know that your entire body has been worked on. You may notice a change in things that I haven't even said. And as Sheri places all the healing energy in, she is touching your entire body. Now I feel like I can be very calm and allow everything to just be at peace within."

Sheri says, "I feel that you have this magnetic field around your body. It's like an Etch-a-Sketch toy—you can see wherever the magnets move. That is what I feel as I move my hands around you, placing energy in your body. Sometimes I feel it a little stronger in different places but it is almost equal everywhere. It is very strong."

Debra says, "I have my hands now over my head so I am pencil-straight, making sure that your lines and your meridians and your strands and everything inside of you are aligned. It is rebalanced and in tune; it is flowing in this new frequency that is harmonious for your body. But I do feel pressure in both my temples, like a light headache, and it's probably just there because they worked on the head to change the vibration and the frequencies. Spiritually, emotionally, and physically, you went through all of these. And when we do that, it's a shift. But because you are not used to doing this, it can make you really tired.

"I feel the presence of your mother in-law. (Annette's mother-in-law passed just days prior to this session.) I recognize her by her laugh; I just heard her cackle. She is in a good space, she is happy and she wants you to know that it is full of joy there. When I mention her name, there was immediate pain in my heart, so I know your heart is hurting. So we heal your heart from all the pain and the sorrow that you have had to deal with. Know that God is giving your heart strength. All is well. All is well there and all is well here for you."

Debra says her temples really hurt, and she asks Sheri work on this area. Sheri says, "Do you want me to actually physically touch? I have so much energy in my hands, so I am going to place them on both sides of her temples. So just breathe, relax, and feel the energy going in."

Debra pauses, then says, "I can feel God's presence."

Sheri says, "I just started crying right before you said God entered," as she also felt the presence of God. Her hands remain on Annette's temples and she continues, "I can feel His hands on you."

Debra says, "I can feel Him in the room. I can feel His love. It is being infused within you. Feel it. If you feel the need to cry about anything that is worrying you, anything that you have gone through, or just even the gratitude of feeling your Father in the room, now is the time. For it is His hands that are placed on your forehead and temples, on your head, for it is His touch and His favor that He puts into you. So with this gratitude we give Him thanks. God just bent down and He kissed your forehead."

Debra continues, "With that, I want you to seal this healing with God's light and love. And when Sheri takes her hands off, you might feel like you got lighter, almost dizzy. That is the energy change you felt. So we give thanks to our Father for coming into this room, for holding your hand, for giving the words, for placing His hands on you, for the healing, for using us as His instruments, but more importantly for you, Annette, because you are the one who came here." Sheri then leaves the room to get Lisa. The session ends with all of the women holding hands and reciting the Lord's Prayer. Everyone is crying.

⚜ ⚜ ⚜

Debra and Sheri received this email from Annette's daughter Lisa on May 23, 2014:

I just want to start off with saying how very grateful my family and I are for the two of you and the gift of healing you have given my mother. Since that evening that she spent with you, a true miracle–or should I say miracles–has been performed. She left that evening a different person. She left with peace of mind, courage, and strength. The following week she went for a needle biopsy for the two lesions that were found on her lungs, only to be told there was nothing there to biopsy. Miracle number one! Yesterday she had her surgery to have the mass in the outer wall of her rectum removed. She was originally told that due to the size of the mass she would need a permanent colostomy bag and that following the surgery she would need radiation and chemo. To the doctor's surprise, the mass had shrunk. Miracle number two! Therefore she did not need a colostomy bag. Miracle number three! Nor will she need chemo. Miracle number four! Praise the Lord for this divine intervention! God is good! And thank God for the two of you! We love you, Debra and Sheri! Thank you ~ the Puleo girls xoxo

Debra and Sheri received this text from Annette's daughter Lana on June 5, 2014:

Hi Debra and Sheri, it is Annette Puleo's daughter in New York. I just wanted to again thank you for the miraculous spiritual healing you provided to my mother. She had a follow-up appointment today with her doctor and was told the original size of the tumor was 6 cm. When they operated on her, they found the tumor was only 1.2 cm, a true miracle. God is so good! We truly feel very blessed. Thank you again! Eternally grateful, Lana Puleo.

Annette Puleo's testimonial and final doctor results after her healing session:

In April 2014 I was diagnosed with a recurrence of endometrial cancer. A needle biopsy of the tumor and a PET scan confirmed this diagnosis. The scan also revealed large lesions on my lung. Additionally, the scan revealed a mass in the rectum approximately 5.7 centimeters in length. After this scan my oncologist told me I would need surgery, which would include a permanent colostomy, radiation, and chemotherapy. I was devastated. My daughter then took me to Debra and Sheri for a healing. I felt very anxious and nervous prior to the healing.

When I left the healing that night I felt an emotional and spiritual calm come over me. Four days later I had to have a pre-op CT scan for my lungs with a possible needle biopsy. The CT scan was negative for lesions, and no biopsy was needed. I was later examined by a second surgeon who said the tumor was not so big and I probably would not need a permanent colostomy. My surgery took place on May 22, 2014. The tumor measured 1.2 centimeters. I had a resection of part of the colon–no colostomy, no chemotherapy, just radiation.

Thank you, God, Debra, and Sheri.

P.S. During my healing session, Debra experienced an allergic reaction to a medication called sulfa. Many years ago I had an allergic reaction to this very medication. I was amazed that she experienced this without any knowledge of my allergies.

# Chapter Fifteen

## Addressing the Overwhelming Pain from Suicide

### Dr. Judith Miller Healing Session
### April 30, 2014

Judith Miller was born and raised in a small town in Arizona to blue-collar parents. She figured out early on that the way out of near-poverty was through education. Judith attended Arizona State University on full academic scholarship. Upon graduation, she began working in a laboratory where she met the man who would become her husband. It was at his encouragement that she entered medical school and became a doctor.

The years flew by as Judith practiced medicine and happily devoted her energy to raising their two sons. But tragedy struck when the boys were teenagers: Judith's husband committed suicide. Since that time, all of her energy has been spent helping her boys heal and move forward in their lives with a sense of peace and security while she continues to deal with the pain and suffering from the loss of her husband.

The Healing Session
Debra begins, "The moment you stepped in this room, I felt as though something was activated. I was receiving information but I could not yet share it. I know there are multiple things that are going to happen. I taste medicine going up my nose and I can taste it in my throat, which means it's being

administered in my arm. I also felt some more medicine go through my veins that makes my body feel heated inside. It was given to you to help you relax, to warm you throughout.

"My neck is becoming really straight. I feel a lot of pressure on my shoulders. I have a lot of pressure on the side of my neck. I can't move my neck and it feels like it is locked down. It is making my spine straight.

"Everything is being aligned. You're off balance. We need to get you realigned, recentered. Your body is getting an attunement. Then things will become clearer. Doors will open and some will close but you will be grateful for those that close. Even if at first you think, *Oh my gosh, why did that door have to close?* But you will see things differently. So we fine-tune so that your body can be on the right vibration, the right frequency for what you need to tune yourself.

"I am feeling lots of pressure on my chest. It hurts, and it burns. I can feel it radiating—this is everything that you hold. It all goes onto your chest. That's where you hold worry and pain. What you hold on your chest makes me want to cry, for I feel it. You hold so much responsibility. And then it hurts you throughout your body. Sometimes your throat is so dry because you can't speak it but you hold on to it.

"Now I am feeling soreness in my right arm between the two bones. I don't know if this is caused from something prior. I feel that they are massaging it. The spiritual surgeons are going to go everywhere in your body even if it is just an ache or something that needs to be manipulated.

"I want you to feel the presence, this coolness that is coming into the room; it feels like it is surrounding the outer shell of your body. You can feel it entering your left side. It gives you this chill inside, an overwhelming feeling. I want you to feel the presence entering the room and know that it is God.

"He stands here and He says, 'Why do you hold all the responsibility? Why are you holding it all? There is no need. There is no need. I am here for you to give me that responsibility. You can't be supermom, the superhero. Some things we just have to let play out. We can't fix them. And we question all the whys because they destroyed everything that you knew. I am here to hold your hand.'"

Debra says, "I feel He is holding your left hand, and He looks down at you and He says, 'Everything has taken place for you and each individual in your family to become who they are, to have a new understanding, to have a new awareness.' Some things have to be hard for us in order for us to see. But if you give it to God and you trust that no matter what you do, if you just walk through it, you are going to be okay. Don't put so much pressure on yourself. Look at things with a different attitude like, 'I may not understand why it's happening but I trust it.' It's freeing and it lifts the burdens off of you." Debra says she keeps hearing the words *Let it go. Let it go. Let it go.*

Debra continues, "As you lie here, you are connected by a cord to each of your children. And these cords that we hold on to affect us. That is why we have emotion when they have emotion. That's why we feel sadness when they feel sadness. We feel happy when they feel happy because we have a cord that connects. What I am here to tell you is that when one is healed, you are all healed. So what God is placing in you will also be placed in them. This is His light, and His truth, and His love. They each feel it, each will acknowledge it, and each will own it. But it is up to them to become one with it. But God will give each of them what you receive today for He hears your prayers.

"I want you to relax and know that your body is being worked on because we are going to work on healing the mind and the heart at the same time. The mind has to go through so much turmoil and ask so many questions, but the heart has to go through all the pain. The heart holds everyone else's pain. We heal this emotion that is connected between both. We allow the healing and the energy to take out what doesn't need to be there. Imagine pulling a sword out of your heart and then suturing the hole with God's light and love; ta[...] out the hurt but filling it with this new light. So while these areas are being worked on, we are going to take a spiritual journey.

"I will be leading you on this guided spiritual journey. And you may see it in your mind or you will feel as if you are floating weightlessly above your body. Don't be afraid and drop back down; stay in that mode where you feel light, weightless, and disconnected from your body. As you do this you are able to float out. It's like a balloon that slowly goes up, so effortlessly, so smoothly, so beautifully, so easily.

"As we go up we are going to a space where we are going to see and connect differently. The balloon is still going up, we are following that balloon, and as we do I feel a little pressure in my head. Pressure in my forehead, this is okay. Just relax. There you go. Then I have your hand, my left hand holds your right hand and we are there. We did it. And you smile. You are like, *Okay, now what?*

"As we walk forward it's like a new experience, it's like walking in the dark. What are we going to bump into, what are we going to see? It's like a mystery but magical. All of a sudden ahead of us is this trail that we are walking on. It is made of this beautiful light. It's as if there is an arch. We are going to go through the arch and then we are surrounded with this white light. We are standing in it, surrounded by it, we are breathing it, holding it, becoming one with it. This is God's light. It feels as if there is a thick veil that stands in front of us. We can't see the veil; the veil is this bright light."

Debra knows what she is seeing ahead. She has been to and through the veil many times. She says, "There is someone coming through. God is pushing through and allowing us to stand on one side of the veil and allowing the loved one to come through the other side of the veil. He stands in front of you. This is your husband. This is how you remember him. He looks pure, he looks healthy, and he looks perfect. There is some anger that you have. How can you be so perfect and so happy and so healthy and leave me with all the burdens and the weight and the struggles? How can you be here with no struggles, no pain, and filled with love?

"As he stands there, you have these feelings going back and forth. He hears them. God steps in. God is on your left, holding both of you, putting one hand on each of your shoulders. He looks at you and He says, 'Do not be mad at him. Do not be mad. This was not his fault. This was what overcame him. There was a darker side, an illness that overcame him like a shadow. I took this shadow out and he is now light. So don't be mad at him. Forgive him. He did not ask for that shadow. That was part of his journey. As he puts his hand on you, he is trying to allow you to forgive.'"

Debra tells Judith that it is okay to cry. "Know that this was orchestrated and watched by God. And your husband says, 'I did not mean to abandon you. There was no thought process, this was not thought through and I see things differently from here. And I had to go through my own healing. I am sorry for all that you have endured, for all the pain and pressures that I put you and the boys through. But I still love you.' God says, 'Do not be mad at him. Do not be mad at him.'" Debra feels that Judith is having a hard time forgiving and this is why God is repeating His words.

"Look at him. Look at him now. Feel his love. Feel his sorrow. For this is giving healing for all, not just you but for your boys too. Do not be mad. God is going to give you a vision. The vision I see is your husband, sick and dying in a hospital bed. God has you look at him dying and he has no last words, and there is no reason, and there is no cause and the doctors can't figure out why. But he dies. Will you hold him at fault? Will you be angry with him? It's the same. So as your husband stands here in front of you, God is there."

Debra continues, "I can still feel your anger, Judith. It hurts so much in your heart that it's like thorns are woven around it.

So we are working on the heart to release this pain, to be free and to be able to forgive. You are going to have to say the following words and repeat them in your mind. So please repeat them after me.

"I know that God is standing there with His hands open and your hands placed on His and you're going to say these words to Him. If you want a visual, look into the eyes of the picture of Jesus on the wall. Say these words now in your mind: 'I am angry, I am hurt, I feel left alone, I carry all the weight. I no longer want this burden, I no longer want to feel this pain. I release this to you, God, and as I do and as you heal my heart, and as I really give these words to you, I know I am doing it for my sons too. So with all my heart, I am begging you to take this burden and this pain away now. I no longer need it, I no longer want it, I no longer want to hold it. Please take this from me, I no longer deserve it.'"

Debra, Sheri, and Judith cry as they feel all the emotions from God's love to the release of Judith's pain. Debra says, "God puts His hands on your head and He holds your head and He says, 'This was not your fault, this was part of this journey that you are on. It's up to you now to stand in my light and create a new journey, one full of light and love and freedom, now that your heart is healed.'"

Debra adds, "God gives all of this to you here and now. Everyone has their own journey. We cannot control each and every journey. We cannot control our children's journeys. We can guide them, we can love them, we can pray for them, and we can send this love and energy to them. But this is not your responsibility beyond this point. They are the ones who need to want it, and walk it, and breathe it. So I want you to look down as if you are seeing your oldest son. And I want you to see that beam of light that locked you down on this table, but now we are going to take that beam of light and we are going to surround your son.

like a light bulb glowing over him, and it shields and
protects him and loves him, heals him, holds him. And as you
see that, God says, 'Look at me. That was God's light, my light
that I am shining on him and I am within him. So you need
to give the worry to me, for I will be the one who is responsible for him.' It is no longer your responsibility or your worry.
Then you feel pressure in your mind, *How can a mother not
worry? How can a mother not have responsibility?* God says, 'Worry
will do you no good.' We can't be responsible for their actions.
But we can place this in God's hands, knowing that whatever
happens is God's will and this frees you from worry and that is
what God wants to do.

"As you stand there, we place white light on you, around
you, within you, letting you feel the love and the connection
that you can have each and every day. This light doesn't go
dim, it shines brightly. Remember the path that you and I
took; it looked dark and then through the arch there was so
much light. That's your new path. You are now surrounded in
this light. So get through the hurdles, but see them as good,
see the blessings in everything, even if it doesn't look like it,
knowing that each step is leading you down this new journey,
into this new beginning that is so bright for you.

"God shows me that you are laughing in your future and
you're smiling and you're in love again. For you deserve it and
it is coming to you. So as we turn around and we leave the veil,
we come down back into our bodies, into this room. Looking
down through the top of your head and down through your
body, I feel warm. I see clearness. I want to make sure everything is functioning in unison and that there are no blockages
in you and that this white light is swirling through you. I felt
a little pinch right above my knee as I was saying the swirls of
white light were going through you–there was a little blockage
and I could feel it break through. Sheri is placing sheets of
energy all around your body and it is going around you, inside
you, over you, and through you.

"Since you were aligned and recentered, you will have a new attunement and awareness. You will see things more clearly. It is your job now to light a candle before you start or end your day. Connect, and have your direct connect to God. Release any worry, any of the things that burden you. For we all have things every day that burden us or weigh us down or distract us; we release that knowing that all is well. When you get used to doing it daily, it helps us release the control. If we release the control, it is all in God's control, and if He is the one who is leading and guiding and protecting us, then we really can't go wrong.

"But some type of spiritual surgery took place to mend your heart, your arm, and other areas. Sheri worked on your body while we were having our journey. When I tasted the medicine I knew something big was taking place. Acknowledge this because I feel you might be tired, so honor this, and allow the healing to continue."

Sheri asks Judith if she has any questions. Judith says, "No, it was all spot-on." She begins to weep. "Everything that I have been thinking about, it was spot-on, all the thoughts, all the pain, all of it."

Debra says, "God knows you. He hears you and He wants to take this pain away. It took God to release this. But as you release right now and you cry right now, you're healing your son too."

Sheri adds, "That is so powerful."

Judith continues, "I loved this man so much. To see him destroyed like he was, how you talked about that darkness that descended. I saw it, I knew when it came down. There was nothing I could do to save him."

Sheri says, "We are human and it's too big for us."

Judith replies, "It just happened and it tortured him. He hated himself. It was just so hard. And then for him to put a bullet into his head was a relief."

Debra says, "It took the pain away."

Judith says, "He was angry but he dropped it all on me. The mess, the pain, the abandonment, the kids–it was all just dropped on me. And I didn't deserve that. I was a good wife. I loved him through everything; all of his struggles, all of his pain, I loved him. I didn't deserve to be treated like that."

Sheri responds, "There was so much lifted from your heart. It was pulled out. There was a lot pulled out."

Judith says, "It's funny, the day that it happened I felt such chest pain. The diagnosis was that the heart literally doesn't function due to emotional pain. I have been coming back from that."

Debra adds, "It's like thorns wrapped around your heart." Sheri and Judith agree.

Sheri says, "Debra, can you come up from under the table now; I want to end in the Lord's Prayer. I feel the presence of God." Debra confirms His presence as she feels very cold. Sheri is crying but continues, "As I was standing here I felt like I was your husband, holding your hand so tightly, and I just felt the love. I felt it so much, I felt it was him."

Judith says, "I love him so much."

Debra asks, "Did you see him healthy?"

Judith answers, "I actually did. One night he came to me in my dreams and he was the man that I married. He comes up to me and tries to reach out to me but I was angry and said, 'Don't touch me, you don't deserve to touch me, don't touch me!' But he said, 'I miss you so much.' I pray every day to give him forgiveness. Sheri and Debra, you did this today. I know I can't ask for forgiveness until I am willing to forgive."

Debra says, "Remember this day. You said those words to God."

Debra, Sheri, and Judith blow out the three candles, ending the healing session. Everyone in the room is crying.

⚜ ⚜ ⚜

Dr. Judith Miller Testimonial:
On the morning of December 26, 2010, my husband of thirty years told me that he was running out to Starbucks to get our morning coffee. I told him I would just make coffee at home as our son had given us Starbucks coffee for Christmas. He insisted, so I acquiesced. About fifteen minutes later, I received a frantic phone call from my sister and then one from his sister. I became panicked and I was flooded with a horrible feeling as I heard sirens in the distance.

A police car pulled up to our house. I watched the officer walk up to the house. He needed no words; the expression on his face said it all. My beautiful husband had driven to an empty parking lot and committed suicide. Before he pulled the trigger, he had called 911 to inform them where to find him, so that we would be spared the discovery of what he had done.

Our world came crashing down. I couldn't breathe; my heart felt as if it were about to explode. Our beautiful boys were devastated. I went through the motions of closing down our home and relocating to Arizona, where my older son was in college. I had a desperate need to keep us together; I was afraid that we would fragment in our grief if we were apart.

We went to grief counseling. For four months I spent hundreds of dollars per week for counseling for the three of us. My younger son quit first. I soon followed. I had no answers and no closure. I couldn't sleep at night and spent hours channel surfing. One late night, I came across the program *Long Island Medium*. I was instantly mesmerized with the idea of contacting a medium in an effort to get some closure, to help with the crushing pain of the suicide since suicide provides no answers for those left behind. There is just grief, questions, and more grief and questions.

I turned to the internet and that is where I found Debra Martin. It took me three months of wrestling with myself, but I finally made an appointment to attend one of her sitting circles. I arrived with picture in hand, as per her request. When it came time to speak to me, she told me something that she had no way of ever knowing–that my husband was glad that I had kept him with us, he wanted to be no other place. She continued to tell me things that she had no way of knowing: that he was the glue that had held us together, that my older son was struggling so much with his father's death. I didn't come away with any answers, but I did come away feeling less alone, feeling that my husband was still there with us.

Three years went by. Each day we continued to move forward. Each day I came to accept what had happened. My mind became clearer, but my heart was so heavy. The pain and burden never lessened. I just got better at compartmentalizing it and making it through the day somewhat intact. When I gave up grief counseling, I turned to prayer and meditation. Every morning I started my day with a prayer of gratitude. I thanked God for everything that was good in my life and I begged God to envelope my husband in His love and light, to help him repair the damage in his soul that led him to take his own life.

My thoughts once again turned to Debra Martin. I had continued to receive her emails and knew that she had begun spiritual healing with a partner who could feel spiritual energy. I again had this nagging, recurring, lingering thought that took hold and just wouldn't go away. Once again, after three months of wrestling with the idea, I made an appointment. I wasn't sure what the outcome would be, but I couldn't and wouldn't let go of the idea. To be honest, I was desperate to try anything. I knew I couldn't live my life in constant emotional pain. I was willing to try anything that would bring some relief to this horrific pain that just would not go away.

We started our session by lighting our candles. Debra then led me to a table where I was to lie peacefully as she and Sheri conducted our session. I closed my eyes, and the first words that I heard from Debra were the exact words that I use to start my morning prayer: "Hear my prayer, O Lord, hear my prayer…" This went on for the whole session–I would hear my prayer echoed back to me in my exact words. I was instructed to forgive too, and that the burden that I carried was not mine alone. I cried silently, but felt the forgiveness and burden lift from me. The whole session was intensely personal and very healing. After the session, Debra, Sheri, and I just held each other, hugging, laughing, and crying. I felt instantly connected to them in so many ways. I thanked them and begged them to continue their work, for I know that their work has also cost them in many ways. There is so much skepticism and cynicism in the world in regards to their work.

In closing, I will state that I am a physician, educated in the hard sciences. I have been in practice for fifteen years. I have had to pronounce patients when they died. In spite of my hardcore education, I have never lost my belief in the soul. I have walked into a room after a patient has passed and have felt his spirit in the room. I have felt the presence of the spirit and have felt the presence of God. I am so thankful that there are people like Debra and Sheri who minister to that spirit.

"Lose all your control. Give it to God. When you let God have all the control, you will never be led wrong. It's very freeing when you surrender your control to God, knowing He will lead the way. It may not always be easy but He will give you the strength. When you surrender your control, God will make very clear what you are supposed to do. You will not have any doubt. It will be very clear. You won't be able to deny it. Therefore you will do it. Trust the open and closed doors." – Debra and Sheri

# Chapter Sixteen
# Trusting that God is the One in Control

**Teresa Lewis Healing Session**
**May 28, 2014**

Teresa Lewis was born April 20th, 1959, the third child in a family of five. She grew up in a middle-class neighborhood in Farmington Hills, Michigan, and attended Northern Michigan University. She then moved to Arizona where she and her husband raised their four children. Eventually Teresa had six grandchildren who knew her as Meme. She doted on her family and "Sundays at Meme's" was a weekly event that everyone enjoyed. Teresa worked at Phoenix Children's

Hospital for twelve years, earning the respect and love from everyone she worked with.

Twelve years ago, Teresa was diagnosed with systemic scleroderma. She was in pain much of the time but never complained. Only her husband, mother, and sister really knew the pain she suffered.

Teresa and her mother and sister were extremely close. They saw each other often and talked on the phone several times a day. When her mother died, Teresa was inconsolable. For her fifty-fifth birthday, Teresa's sister, Pati, gave her a gift of a reading with Debra Martin, thinking it would bring much-needed healing to her broken heart.

The reading on May 15th, 2014, was more than Teresa could have hoped for. Her mom, dad, and an aunt came through loud and clear and she was very excited about what the future would hold for her, knowing that her mom would always "have her back."

Less than a week later, Teresa had a small fever and a sore back. Her fever was gone by Monday, but her back still hurt. On Tuesday the doctor ordered an MRI, thinking she had a slipped disc, but on Wednesday she was admitted to the hospital and within an hour doctors discovered she had a bad infection that had turned septic. Because of the scleroderma, Teresa was on immune suppressors. Thus a small infection that any of us would have fought off in a day took over her body. One hour later she was sedated and placed on life support. She never regained consciousness.

One week later, Debra and Sheri received an email from Teresa's daughter, Nicole Lewis: "My mother saw you on May 15th for a reading. Her name is Teresa Lewis. She is in ICU on life support now. Can you do healings for this critical of a condition? Please let me know. Thank you." Attached to the message was a photo of Teresa.

Sheri immediately started sending healing energy to Teresa. A healing was scheduled for Teresa's daughter Nicole on May 28th.

On the night before the scheduled healing, Debra and Sheri called Nicole and said that they felt that they had to come to the hospital right away. They arrived at the hospital wearing temporary tattoos of Spider-Man on their forearms, which had been placed there in honor of a friend who had passed. Teresa's family members noticed the tattoos and told Debra and Sheri that the last thing Teresa had done before falling ill was take her grandson to the Spider-Man movie. They also learned that the case on Teresa's iPad was a Spider-Man web. That Debra and Sheri had arrived sporting those tattoos had great meaning for Teresa's family.

Debra and Sheri entered Teresa's room for prayer and an impromptu healing session. Debra and Sheri held Teresa's hands in the hospital room and explained to her what was going to take place in her healing session the next day. When it was over, Teresa's sister Pati said that she would be praying with her mother the next morning while Nicole had her healing session at the healing center. Debra said that the healing would begin at 11:11 a.m., which held much significance to the family. Teresa had recently shared with them that she felt her mother kept coming to her at 11:11 or 1:11.

The Healing Session

Prior to the healing, three of Teresa's grandchildren place Teresa's photo on the healing table. Teresa's daughter Nicole sits in a chair in the healing room to observe the healing session. Debra starts, "Teresa, we are honored to have you on our healing table. You are here in the healing center on the healing table because we have a picture of you on the healing table. I will lie on the table and be your proxy while you are in the hospital receiving. Last night when we visited you at the hospital we told you that your job is just to receive."

Debra says, "I may meet you in spirit. I may meet you out of body, joining you, speaking with you and you will be overseeing everything as God orchestrates this all. Sheri will anchor me and monitor me at all times so that if I do meet you in spirit, I know that I can effortlessly return. Nicole, we have pictures of Jesus in the room, and if you need to focus you can look at the pictures. The best thing that you can do, Nicole, is just to close your eyes, but also receive this healing because you are here as well. The pain you are going through also needs to be healed. You are here as a proxy for your entire family and so as you sit here with the intentions of miracles for your mother, God is placing His hands on you which means they are placed on everyone in your family."

Debra positions herself on the table and places Teresa's picture on her abdomen. "When the three of us lit the candles today, we all became one. Nicole lit a candle for her mother. Let's let the healing begin." Almost immediately Debra says, "My forehead really hurts. I have a lot of pressure in my head. There is a lot of pressure right in the center of my head. I don't want you to be concerned, but I can see Teresa in this healing room. It just means that her body is being worked on. It doesn't mean that she has transcended, it just means that she can be here because I just saw her full body stand right here in the room. She is overseeing what is to be done. Teresa is anxious to talk, but knows this work has to be done first.

"The tops of my hands are stinging because there is so much heat going through them." Teresa comes to hold Debra's hand like Debra and Sheri did the night before in the hospital. Debra says, "She is so caring." Debra then cries out in pain and says, "The spiritual surgeons are here to do a spiritual surgery." Sheri goes to both of Debra's hands, touching every finger, and to both of her feet, touching every toe.

Debra says, "I can feel the presence of your mom in the room. Your mother is smiling. She just loves these grandchildren so much. My chest is burning. This lung is being heated and being worked on. My whole body is hot right now. I am getting a pinching in my solar plexus and belly button area. I know something is taking place and I see God's beam of white light. I can feel tingling going down my shoulders into my arms. I can feel the flow going through my veins.

"Nicole, as soon as you made the call for the healing, you played a role to get this done. You are going to feel the presence of God in the room right now, standing at the end of the bed. And your mom is here too and she is at the right side of the healing table. They are both here. Normally I see them side-to-side if they do enter. But I see your mom standing up front. She is telling me something. These are words from Teresa. 'We made a commitment to each other, Debra, one that we didn't even realize at the time. It was God's commitment, for the room was filled with witnesses of how it all transpired. You need to trust how everything is being orchestrated and put into alignment.'"

Debra starts to cry and takes a deep breath. "Teresa is holding my hands. Teresa is telling me to take the responsibility away and that it is her turn now to tell me that all is going to be okay. But she is holding both of my hands and looking at me and saying, 'All will be okay, all will be okay.' And this time she says it with such strength, where before I was saying it with such strength. Before, when Teresa attended my healing circle, I felt so strong telling her these words. But still she questioned the words I was saying. I could feel it and see it in her eyes, her pain and her fear. And now she doesn't question and she stands here with pure strength saying, 'All will be okay, don't worry.' This time it is I who am standing here not understanding and questioning. Teresa is giving me a hug. Teresa is walking around the table. She is going over to her daughter. She just kneeled down in front of Nicole."

Debra says, "Please place your hands out in front of you, Nicole." Nicole begins to cry. "Let her hold your hands. She is looking at you. Remember her eyes, she is looking at you. Teresa says, 'All is going to be okay. It is okay.' It is time to cry, this is the place to cry. Let it all out. Let your mom hold your hands as you cry. If you just felt hands behind you on your shoulders, it was God's hands for He stands behind you very tall. As you sit and your mother kneels in front of you, they are now both embracing you. Teresa says, 'It is okay. I am okay. I am at peace. This is only my body. Allow it to heal. Do not fear what I am going through because I don't feel it. I am proud of you and I love you. God holds you tight.'" Through her tears, Nicole says that she felt God physically touch her back.

Debra continues, "He held you really tight. God is squeezing your shoulders like your father would. He kissed the top of your head right now. He says, 'I am the way, I am the truth, I am the life. I hold you. I will give you the strength you need. Trust in me. Your mom is in my care and I bring her forth to you so that you see her whole, so that you are able to feel her love and so that you feel her healthy. This is what you need to place in your mind. This is what you need to place in your family's minds. My mom is healthy. My mom is at peace. That is just my mom's body.'"

Debra says, "So as your mom sits with you holding your hand and God holds your shoulders very tightly, Teresa's body is being picked up. It is standing straight up. It's like the table is being shifted upward. Look how she is aligned under the white light. Her body is transparent. You can see right through the body. All the places that are white, you do not see a body inside. All you see is white. God says, 'That is my light. And as she is tilted up, my white light is beaming through her. She has light throughout her entire body. Imagine placing a light bulb through the top of her head and turning it on and you see the glow radiating outward. Through her hands, through her feet, you can see it glowing through her body. That is my light. That is my light. I am shining through her. That is my light. I see brightness, I see light, I do not see dark.'"

Debra says to Sheri, "I need you to anchor me." Then she adds, "For a brief moment, you guys might feel as if I died. Do not be afraid, do not fear if you do not see me breathing. I may become lifeless so that I can breathe again and have new life." Sheri places her hands over the center of Debra's body to anchor her. The room becomes silent. Debra's head turns to the side and she resembles a rag doll lying lifeless on the table. A long moment of silence passes. Then Debra says softly, "I am seeing from above. Your mom is touching the Universe. They are dancing. Everyone is dancing. They are all dancing." Debra becomes emotional as she describes what she is seeing. "There is a great dance up there. They are celebrating. It is like the final dance, the big hurrah, and the explosion. They are all in white. So many angels, so many spirits. I am walking through it. I am walking through the dance.

"There is some scripture, some writing on this wall that I am seeing. It is gold and it almost looks like Braille. I am touching it with my hand and trying to read it. It is so beautiful. It is a golden tablet. It is like an award, like a certificate, a golden award. They are presenting it in the highest honor. I can see everyone taking their positions.

"I can see in the hospital room as if it is right next to this room. I can see your aunt Pati's head down on the bed as she holds Teresa's hand and prays. I just saw Jesus approach." Debra's voice sounds as if she is about to cry. "I saw His face. He is walking in His robe with it over His head. He is walking slowly, He is walking forward and He takes my hand and He nods His head. I feel like I am moving forward, but it is probably just in spirit. Jesus stands right next to me. Jesus says, 'You are doing the work that I have done. There are many of you, but you have been chosen and I am here to shake your hand.' He reaches down and He puts his hand on Teresa's head. He is putting it on her head as she is kneeling by her daughter. So now you, Nicole, have God behind you, you have your mother on her knees in front of you, and you have Jesus in His robe placing His hand on your mom. 'Glory,' says Jesus.

"Jesus picks your mom up. She is standing. She just kissed you on the cheek. God is still holding you. Jesus has put His arms around Teresa to guide her back." Sheri cries as she continues to anchor Debra, and Nicole sobs in the chair. "They are stepping out, she is walking away. But God is still holding you. It is okay; your mother is not leaving you. She is actually going to go back into her body. We took her out so we could work on the body and now she is going to go back in. She goes back in and she takes a new breath of life, a new beginning."

Debra's arms have been stretched out straight off the table during the time that she was seeing from above. She asks Sheri to put her arms back on the table. Debra says, "I have no movement. My arms are numb. I feel real skinny, like all bone. I can't move my fingers and everything is numb. There are words for you, Nicole. These are God's words. As He holds you, He comes around in front of you. He wants you to stand up." Nicole stands. "He is so big, isn't He? God says, 'You need to trust in me, for I have the power and the light. Do not waver your thoughts. You felt me touch you. I did this so that you knew that what is being done is real. You can't deny it. You felt it. I am here. I am watching. I am healing. This is a process. I will be holding your mother's hand the entire way. Just like I held you and gave you strength, I am holding and putting strength in her hand each and every day. You can sit now.'"

Debra continues, "He places His hands on your shoulders and God says, 'I know you feel that pressure. Don't feel that weight. You are taking on the weight of everyone's emotions and feelings. Give that to me and I will hold it and I will touch each and every one of them. It is not your duty. It is mine. Just remember, Thy will be done on Earth as it is in Heaven.' And with that, God is leaving."

Debra asks Sheri to place a seal around Teresa with God's white light and love. This allows the energy to continue to flow harmoniously to the frequency that she needs. Debra adds, "For when Teresa took her new breath, her first breath, the body shifted. It will no longer be what it was. Everything will be altered, showing her that this is new and restored, rebalanced, recentered, and realigned. But it can no longer be the same. In order to have it new, we had to take everything out and start over. Your job, Nicole, is to pray to God. With this, we give thanks. We give thanks to Pati for believing and trusting in this process and for sending her sister here. God spoke through each one of you. And as you see it all unfold, you can see how God worked through each one of you from the very beginning to the very end and now the healing is done. With this, we give thanks to all who played a role. We give thanks for allowing us to be the instruments of God for this healing right here and now. We give thanks for Teresa for coming and having a connection. And we give thanks to God, to Jesus, to the spiritual surgeons, and to everyone who played their role here today. We are honored. We are humbled. Amen."

Debra asks Nicole to come over to the table and hold hands with her and Sheri and say the Lord's Prayer. The three of them hold hands while Debra is still lying on the table and pray.

Debra says, "As we stand here, we need to put our humanness aside and we have to trust that God is in control and let the worry go. For whatever happens, it is God's will. And we saw and witnessed the beautiful transformation take place and now we get to watch it transpire. Thank you."

⚜ ⚜ ⚜

Teresa passed on May 30, 2014. Her service was held on June 11, 2014, at 11:11 a.m.

Debra and Sheri were saddened by Teresa's passing. But they know that it is not up to them and that it is up to God for He is the one who is in control. It is God and God alone who is the Healer.

# Chapter Seventeen
# Healing is a Process.
# You Have to Feel to Heal.

**Steve Bicknase Healing Session
April 28, 2014.**

In Steve's own words:

I grew up on a farm in southern Minnesota with eight brothers and sisters. We milked cows and raised pigs. I knew that this was not the life for me. I excelled in school and in sports, so I knew that I wanted to go to college.

I went off to college at Mankato State in Minnesota where I decided to become a teacher. In my first semester, I had the honor of meeting my wife Ann. We dated four years, married after graduation, and have been blessed with two beautiful daughters.

After thirty-six years as a teacher and school counselor, I developed several autoimmune diseases. With my health deteriorating, we happened to see Debra and Sheri on a local news station. We were very skeptical and friends advised us not to see them, but after praying about it, we met Debra and Sheri in October 2012. I scheduled a session and purposely did not tell them what was wrong with me. I came out of that session having my sciatic nerve pain and torn right rotator cuff completely healed. The Father was with me and anointed me with Heavenly Water. These ailments have been gone ever since.

My CIDP and fibromyalgia (autoimmune diseases) had been getting progressively worse. In addition, I found out in 2013 that I had a tumor on my pituitary gland. I decided with my wife and daughters to go see Debra and Sheri again. This time, I specifically asked for healing in my areas of need.

The Healing Session

Debra moves under the healing table to become one with Steve and begins speaking. "Steve, if you could put your hands down to your sides, I am feeling that the spiritual surgeons are putting heat into your palms. These are ports. Palms are ports. Especially the right, because I feel they are putting an IV in this right arm. It's going to be very stationary, you are going to feel like you can't move your arms. I am feeling like I can't move my arms. There is a lot of heat going into the arms and also a lot going through the palms. Not only is this white light going through your palms, it is going through your belly button right now. It is also activating your third eye. All access ports are being opened; this is what I am hearing.

"The bottoms of your feet are now open. It's as if they are twisting them open like you open a jar. They are open and we will close them at the end but right now we are opening every port so that this light can beam through your body. Right now you can probably feel heat going into your upper arms, right where your biceps are. This is God's light, light of healing, that is going through and penetrating your arms and going through your ports. My arms cannot move. They are stationed. I know that they have to stay this way, so I will hold them in this position for you."

Debra takes a series of deep breaths. "God is coming into this room. Wow, this is so early into a session and so quickly. He is standing at the top of the healing table. Wow, at first I saw Him come from the bottom of the table and then in a blink I now see Him and His energy at the top of the healing table where your head is. I taste some medicine right now up my nose. So as I am speaking, two things are happening at once: I am feeling my body go through the healing and I am trying to say things as they are coming quickly. As you lie here, you are also now standing over to the left in the back corner of the room. So your spirit, your soul, God has placed over here to the left behind the healing table. You may feel like your body is lifted. I do feel intense heat going into my arms."

Debra coughs as she tastes more medicine being administered. "As your soul/spirit stands over to the left, you see your body lying on the table, but more importantly"–Debra groans and coughs; she feels like a tube just went down her throat–"you see God standing at the head of your table. For it is God that is going to place this healing into you today. I see God standing at the head of the table; you're watching and as His hands are on your shoulders, you see this beam of light. It's like this whole body, this whole shadow, this whole inner shell you just saw become white. You're a man of light. Think of your solar plexus as a door and the solar plexus is your keyhole.

"So I give you the key. This key is yours. And this key will be yours to allow this healing at any time, for this light to permeate through you. Right now all we want is for this light to infuse the entire body from head to toe. Every vessel, every organ, and every cell being infused with this light can alter all things with a blink, like a switch, on and off. God is standing at the head of the table looking down at you. So Steve, if you need a vision of God, I want you to look at the picture of Jesus on the wall and look into the eyes. I want you to connect with the eyes. I want you to know that He is looking at you with pure love. Pure love. And as He looks at you, you see this purple dot flying in front of your eyes.

"That purple dot is going to swirl in your body. It's going to look like a swirling sphere going from your head to your toes. This is God's strength. He gives you strength to walk through this, to get through this and to allow your mind to know that with His strength all things are possible. And I am not meaning strength to deal with what you are dealing with, I mean strength to know that you are walking forth, shedding everything and leaving it behind. So this purple has gone through your body. I can feel pinching up in my left groin. I just received more medicine. So as God is holding His hands on you, He is holding this light and this strength within you, because what is about to occur is not easy on the body. So if this becomes painful or if this becomes hurtful, you need to know that you can get through this.

"So as God holds your body on this beam of light, He is standing there, watching and observing. But we may have to feel, and I am not sure if it is you or just me." Debra sees a spiritual surgeon enter the room. Debra tells Sheri to move to Steve's head to send energy to the area where Debra sees a tumor. "And we are going to insert a little thin tool that looks like a tube, and at the end of the tube is a light, it's a laser. As we go through the center of where this tumor is, we are going through deeper and deeper and deeper. Because we see the surface and yes, this is okay, but we need to get to the root. The root, which is the center of your issue, goes way deep within, way deep. I taste more medicine. So as we slowly pull this out, you visualize a thin root like the root of a tree. We are going to pull this root and we are going to let it come up and we are going to give it to God through that white light. It will go up to heaven where it doesn't touch you or anyone else.

"At this time Sheri is pulling this root out. You are almost getting a little headache right now as it spirals down. I feel pinching in my arm as well as more medicine going in. I can actually feel my arms while we are doing this; they are tingling and getting heavy and heated." Debra groans in pain.

Debra then says to Sheri, "At the same time, I'd like you to pull the toxins out of his mouth. These are things that have been in his body that are not serving him but only causing more complications. When I say more complications, I feel it down in my abdomen and actually my organs. So we need those toxins to come out. And they will come out through his mouth."

Debra continues, "Steve, if you can open your mouth, we will pull all the dark out. I can almost taste it coming up. Anytime you put anything into your body, you need to bless it, for God can alter it to only work where it needs to work so it doesn't do any harm to any other places in your body. My chest feels really heavy. I am having a hard time. As Sheri pulls this out, my chest is getting really heavy." Debra starts coughing and takes deep breaths in and out. "He can close his mouth now. The back of my head hurts; it is also controlling my eyes. This is interesting because my eyes are twitching. I am not feeling any tingling in my arms but I am feeling a lot in my head, in the very back of my head and also the top of my head, a little burning. It is altering what needs to be altered, restoring it to a healthy state. My head feels locked down, heavy to the table where I can't move it while they work on it. It feels as if it is being pushed into the table very hard.

"The bad cells are being taken out and altered to good cells. Then we go to the lower extremities. Know that you are okay. I feel on my lower legs that my skin is expanded. It feels tight. And when it is tight it expands and it actually hurts, like my legs can't get any bigger, in the lower..." The pain makes it difficult for Debra to speak. She breathes loudly for about a minute before continuing. "As they work on your legs which feel numb right now, they are also working on your groin, and they work on your male privates, all in that area, because everything has to be in balance. When one thing is off-balance, it shifts another balance. So we have to balance everything in the body from the mind to the heart, to the cells, to the organs, to the circulatory, to the nerves, and that is why my arms feel like they are hot. I feel like I want to rub them, massage them.

"When you look at your body, it is positioned as if it were on a cross, giving yourself to God, trusting that thy will be done on Earth as it is in heaven. You are lying in perfect form, allowing God to work within. So as the work continues and as Sheri continues placing energy inside you, you're going to have a conversation. And the conversation is with God.

"I just received more medicine. So we are going to continue to let the healing infuse all areas. I feel like the body is being transformed and altered, like you came in this room one way and you leave another. You no longer will be the same. So as you stand to the left of the healing table, you can feel God in the room." Debra's voice starts to shake as she feels overwhelmed by God's presence.

"As your body lies on this beam of light, it is being worked on. You are going to have your conversation. The two of you just walked down to the end of the table, and you turned around. God says, 'Don't turn around, not yet. See what is in front of you: just white light. You don't know what is beyond that white light but you know it is there. That is where I am leading you. I am the light that you are seeing.' Now as you

ound you can see Sheri working on your body. You can
ѕѵѵ ѵѵ∪rything being done on your body. God doesn't want
you to look at the body anymore. He wants you to stand face to
face in front of your Father. I see you place your hands in His
hands. He is holding them, you are nodding your head yes,
waiting to hear what He has to say. God holds you and holds
your hands and you see Him with this big smile. He smiles at
you like a father who has not seen His son for a long time.
With such love, just adores you. He smiles at you."

As God speaks through Debra, her voice changes. It
becomes a softer, very loving tone. "As He holds your hands,
He says, 'Thank you. Thank you for believing. Thank you for
believing in me.' For without this faith, this would not happen. You are the miracle. I am not the miracle, for you are
the one who is holding it. It's up to you. So when God places
His miracles into you, it is you that creates the miracle, for
it is your faith that is standing in front of me. Without that,
the miracle could not take place. It is all faith. Believe. We
don't need to understand why this is happening. We just need
to know that you are standing in front of God and that if a
miracle can take place, it's in your hands. God placed it in
your hands with a big smile because you deserve it.

"You feel so calm and such peace comes over you; there
is no more worry because when we worry we ignite the fear
that lies within us. The more you release the fear and you
release the worry, then you receive this light. He holds you.
Do not forget that He does not stop holding you. So as God
shines brightly through you, you will be a different person.
So it is up to you to own it, to receive it, and then you will
hold this key, this key of knowledge, this key of faith, this key
of belief. And then it is up to you to share with others that
they too can open this door and receive what you did today.
You have been given a mission and a duty to share this key
with others, the key of knowledge, the key of faith, and the
key of hope.

"God infuses you with His light and with His love. And you will feel right now this white light swirling through your entire body like a breath of cool air." Debra makes a swooshing noise. "For it is God's breath that is blowing into you. God tells you to go back into your body for you have a new purpose."

Sheri says, "I am crying because of the presence of God and the love in the room."

Debra says she feels like crying because of the power of what has taken place and the words that were given to Steve. "I want you to know that during the entire healing, your birth father was here, standing over to the right. I thought at one moment God was going to allow you to speak to him or see him, but now wasn't the time. I wanted to let you know that he was here watching, observing, and getting to be part of your healing as a witness.

"I now want you to say these words: 'I no longer own it, I no longer deserve it, it's gone, it's gone now. I am healthy, I am whole, I have been touched by God. He placed His breath and His hands through my entire body, infusing me with His light and His love, altering and shifting everything that was bad into new. I am now a new person. My soul is the same but my vehicle has been changed. I got a new engine. I got a new start.' So as you step inside this new vehicle of yours, enjoy your ride because it's going to be good.

"When the energy is done being placed from head to toe, I would like you, Sheri, to put the seven seals of God's light and love up and down the body. For when we do this, God is sealing you with this healing. It is yours. It is up to you what you do with it. Stand in it, own it, and know you deserve it because God loves you and I know you love God back."

Debra takes some time to take a series of deep breaths. "We give thanks for being God's instruments. We give thanks for God for coming into this room, for placing His hands on Steve and for breathing in Him. We give thanks for the words He shared. We give thanks for Steve for his faith, for coming in, and for him to have this new mission, for him to stand out of his body to allow this work to be done. I have so much gratitude that I could keep speaking, so I give thanks to God for He said the miracle is now given. This is all a process; there is a lot to be done. It could take a total of six months to be completely done. But six months is not a lifetime."

Steve's wife Ann enters the room and everyone holds hands to recite the Lord's Prayer. Debra asks Sheri and Steve if they noticed that her voice changed as she spoke God's words during the healing. Sheri says, "Yes, I could tell, the whole room shifted. I could not stop crying, it's undeniable."

Debra says, "There was a different voice within me. It was a different tone. It felt as if I wasn't even bringing the words forth, they were just coming out. It was different. They felt so smooth but I couldn't repeat one word."

Steve replies, "It was unbelievable."

Sheri asks, "Did you see God?"

Steve answers, "I saw His hands in mine. I didn't want to leave Him."

Debra adds, "Sweetheart, when that happens, it's because you feel love that is so intense that you don't want to leave. You feel happy, you feel love–why would you ever want to go back into that body? But He placed inside of you knowledge and hope."

Sheri adds, "The words were so touching. The presence of God was so beautiful, so much love. As I was looking at you–I could cry right now–so much love. It was so powerful."

Steve says, "So much love, I could feel it."

Debra replies, "It's a beautiful, undeniable feeling that you can't explain because it goes deep within, touching your soul."

⚜ ⚜ ⚜

Steve received a miracle on April 28, 2014. He stepped into his healing one hundred percent, never giving up his hope or his faith, for God told him there would be painful times.

On May 6, 2014, Debra and Sheri received the following email from Steve:

Thanks, ladies:

I remember Him saying it will take up to six months; being weaker and wobblier and in severe pain is challenging but I have no doubt that God is healing me. Reassurances from my family and friends, plus God's guidance, help me get through the tough times. You two are like extended family to me and your kind words of support are very much appreciated. My faith is unwavering. Let me know what I can do for you two at any time.

God Bless. Steve

On August 30, 2014, Debra and Sheri received this email from Steve:

During my healing, God was in the room with me and filled me completely with love. He wants the world to know how much He loves them. He said that for six months I would have a lot of pain and suffering, but not to be discouraged because I would be healed. This month I had my appointment with my neurosurgeon and he had me do an open MRI. After looking at it, he said he could not see a tumor. The MRI I had in April around the 24th showed my tumor to be at 4.8 millimeters. My neurosurgeon wanted to be sure, so he had me do a closed MRI because it is much more accurate. I just found out that there is no tumor on that MRI either.

Closing words from Steve:

This summer has been very difficult and trying as God said it would be, but He has taken my tumor away. It is not October yet and I do suffer with my autoimmune diseases, but I know that our Blessed Father does heal people and I know that He loves us all and wants us to be happy. I give Debra and Sheri all the blessings in the world. God the Father and His son Jesus have blessed these two ladies to be servants in the Father's army to help people here on Earth.

"Give this worry to me. Count on me for your finances. I will open doors that need to be opened. I will close doors that need to be closed. If you trust in me to be your power, to be your provider, then I am the one who will meet your needs."
- Debra and Sheri

# CHAPTER EIGHTEEN
# PEACE BEFORE PASSING

**Dina Horvath Healing Session**
**June 16, 2014**

Dina Horvath was born on January 12, 1969, in Lompack, California. She was married to Tony Horvath, her best friend, for twenty-three and a half years. Their wedding song was "Dream" by Aerosmith. She liked making jewelry, reading, and watching psychic shows, but she loved spending time with family and friends. Her favorite time of the year was Christmas. Her favorite songs were "I Want to Fly Away" by Lenny Kravitz and "Sweet Child O' Mine" by Guns & Roses. Her favorite movie was *The Wedding Singer*. She was a big hockey fan and always cheered for her favorite team, the Los Angeles Kings.

Dina came to the healing center because she was in the care of hospice at her home. Her doctors had stopped all treatment for her breast cancer. Her aunt Lee contacted Debra and Sheri through email on June 10, 2014, because Dina had wanted to connect with her dad before passing. Lee told Debra and Sheri that Dina had been given two weeks to live and requested a healing as soon as possible.

On June 16th, Dina, her husband, Tony, and her two sisters arrived at the healing center for Dina's session. Dina could not lie on the healing table so she stayed in her wheelchair in the healing room for the entire session. Debra lay on the healing table right next to Dina and Sheri worked around her wheelchair when sending Dina energy. The entire family gathered around Dina prior to the start of her session and said a prayer, placing the healing in God's hands. Her husband and sisters then went to the waiting area with intentions of pure love being sent to Dina during her session.

The Healing Session

Debra kneels next to Dina's wheelchair and holds her feet as Sheri stands behind Dina and holds her shoulders. The three of them connect and become one. Debra says, "Dina, we are honored to have you here in our healing room." She notices that Dina's cheeks are wet with tears and says, "This is the time to cry. Crying is healing when you feel the presence of God. This is the place to release. This is the place that you feel safe. This is what we want. Sheri and I are here for you. This is your time.

"I will guide you and there might be a time where you just feel so relaxed and I might say, 'Dina, we are going to go to that light.' I am going to show it to you and I am going to hold your hand. I am going to guide you. I am going to give you a glimpse of what you are going to see. We are going to take a little journey. I will show you how. Sometimes people can actually go there and others can just visualize the words I am telling them in their minds. Either way, there is no wrong or right way. Sheri will keep us anchored in this room as we take this journey. Sheri holds the energy in this room and you can effortlessly leave and effortlessly return. When loved ones come into the room, I will tell you who they are and I will tell you what they have to say. When God comes into the room, you will know as there will be a shift in the room and you may feel like crying. I will explain it all.

"God will use Sheri's hands to place the healing where you need it." Debra then lies on the table next to Dina. Debra tells Dina that she can connect with the picture of Jesus on the wall if she needs a visual. Debra says to Dina, "You are safe and you are loved and God is putting His white light and love in you. You can feel that love. It makes your chest feel heavy. I can feel it. And then you become relaxed and almost melt into your chair where you really can't feel your feet or your hands. You are just totally relaxed. Just breathe and relax as your heart rate is going a bit fast." Dina admits that she is a little bit nervous.

Debra continues, "We are just calming it down and connecting with the energy that Sheri is sending to you. When I first started connecting with you, the whole left side of my jaw hurt. There is another beam of light coming and that beam of light is going to the center of your chest. It's as if you are opening this area and this white light is beaming through the center of your chest. When it does that, not only does light go in, but we are going to get it so it beams out as well. Right now God is opening the center of your chest to put the white light in. That white light is healing. It is penetrating everything inside of the chest walls with God's love."

Debra says she is getting a stomach cramp. It feels like a stomachache in the belly button area. She is feeling a lot of pressure, cramping, and soreness right there. "We don't want your body to be in discomfort. We don't want you to feel pain, so we are asking God to place this white light like a spiral, going through your entire body and touching everything. It is swirling around so that you can be pain free and so that you can be at peace. When that happens we have to take out the toxins that are within, anything that is not making you feel good. And they are strands. I can see these strands coming through your belly button. God is taking out what you don't need in your body. In your mind you are telling God, *Yes, thank you. Thank you for taking out of my body what it doesn't need and what it doesn't deserve.*"

Debra says, "I can feel such pain in my abdomen when this is happening." She lets out a moan of pain and then takes a deep breath. Debra then asks Dina if she feels the coolness that just came into the room. "It surrounded you and now it is on your left side. That is God. God is here and is standing in the room next to you. That makes you want to cry because you can feel the presence." Debra says this with a change in her voice and she cries as she speaks. Dina and Sheri also have tears rolling down their cheeks as the energy has just shifted in the room and they all feel God's unconditional love.

Debra says, "He stands there right by your feet in the corner. He looks so big, so big and He comes there for you instead of you going there for Him. All you see is this white robe and hands and now you see the face. He looks very much like Jesus. He looks at you with this contentment. I just got medicine up my nose so I know you are receiving some medicine. When that happens, it means that God is going to send someone for some type of spiritual surgery on you. We have two things going on at one time. They are actually going to work in your throat and in your chest."

Debra then says she hears a loud, high-pitched ringing in her right ear. "That is just because they are setting your vibration, your frequency so that you can hear and connect to your loved ones. That was very intense. We go back to the coolness in the room, God being here for you. I want you to envision that you are not in the wheelchair right now, but you are standing in front of Him. And I just heard you say, 'Wow, I look so tiny. I look so thin.' And you are. You are just this little girl and you look so little. You are looking at Him and He holds your hands, Dina. He is holding your hands and He says, 'Do not be afraid. Do not be afraid.' And you can feel your right hand almost burning by your thumb. It feels like a burning sensation. God is holding your hands and He says, 'No one passes without me. I am always there. I am always there.'

"I am going to take you somewhere and I want you to take a deep breath. You are going to let it out three times and you are going to let your mind go to this space where you are standing with God. Then God is going to guide us, okay?

"Here we go, three deep breaths. And you relax and you can see the vision of you, a shadow of you. It is like your soul standing there and right beside you, you see this white robe. This powerful energy, this powerful man, this being, and He places His hand on your lower back and He guides you. I am going to be right behind you, observing. And God says we are going to go up. I am feeling a little dizzy, a little weightless. I do feel a little loopy like I did have medicine administered to me. And as we rise up, you are really not seeing yourself anymore, you are just feeling what I am explaining to you. You are just rising and you are going higher and higher and higher. You see this light that is getting brighter and brighter and brighter.

"As we go to that light, we come to a stop. It is like there is a little piece of pavement, a rock, and a stepping-stone. We see that path ahead of us and it looks like a cloud, like a white fog. Do I go past that fog or do I stay right here? God has got you and His hand is behind you. I am feeling very overwhelmed like I want to cry." She begins to cry, as do Dina and Sheri. "And He says, 'That is where you will go when it your time. You will meet me and we will walk through that haze, that light. But instead of you walking there, I am going to bring someone through heaven to meet you right here.'"

Debra is very emotional as she speaks these words. "And as you are standing there, God brings forth a loved one for you. He is coming and he is getting clearer and clearer to you as he is getting closer. It is your dad. God is letting your dad come through. He looks so healthy and so vibrant and so full of life and so happy, and he hugs you and he holds you and he embraces you. And he has your dog with him! He has this little dog come through that doesn't leave his side. So Dad is here and you remember him by his eyes and you connect with his eyes. He is looking at you eye to eye and you can feel his personality and his love and you know that it is him. He looks at you and he says, 'This is far greater than you will ever know. And I am here.' And now guess who is coming–there is another loved one coming and it is your mom. She comes from the right and she is standing behind. She says she is sorry. She has to say sorry for something and I don't know what the sorry is for, but you understand."

Dina nods her head and says, "Yes."

Debra continues, "And your dad continues to hold you and says, 'We can do great things up here. Everything that you see on Earth, you see in heaven, but it is more vibrant, it is more beautiful. Everything is touchable. I have been watching you and I have been with you. You know that I came to you at your bedside. You knew I was there.'"

Debra says, "You knew he came. I'm not sure if this was in the hospital. You knew he was there. It was very quick and you questioned it in your mind. *Was that my imagination?* Your father says, 'No, I have always been there. I have always watched you. I have always taken care of you, always observing and loving you. That is the one thing that never stops: love.' Your dad takes your hand and says, 'Look down.' As you look down, you are like, *Wow*. It looks like an open canyon, there's nothing below. Your dad says, 'Anything that you want to see is below; it is like electricity. Think of it and it appears. You don't have to go to it. It comes to you. Do not be afraid.'

"Your dad kind of holds your hands and he squeezes them. So he does this thing like one, two, three, squeeze. I don't know why he is doing that. I don't know if I am supposed to make you aware of feeling this so that you will continually know that he is here with you. It's knowing his energy is there. It's a knowing, a feeling where you can't see but you felt like you had to look to the right and he was there. That is the feeling you will have to know that he is still with you. God is still here and God is saying..." Debra says she feels like crying before she even says the words from God. "'Dina, I will have your dad come to you when it is time. He will hold your hand. He will come to you on Earth in your room.'

"Every step of the way, you will be held in God's light. You will walk just like we did going up, rising up effortlessly and so peacefully. And you will have this smile on your face and you will say, 'I am ready.' But until then don't be afraid. There will be no pain. We are healing you from that. It will be effortless. What your body goes through will not be what you feel. You will smile. You will see your dad in the room. He will come to get you. He will guide you just like he did when he guided you down the aisle when you were married."

Debra cries as she says the words, and Dina and Sheri are also in tears. Everyone is overwhelmed by the words and the love in the room. Debra continues, "He is going to bring you home." She cries so much that she can barely say God's words. "'Just like he walked you to the altar, he is going to walk you to my altar, to my gates.' It is a celebration for you. I can see it! It is such a celebration for you. The angels are going to be singing. It will be the happiest day, like your wedding day, remember that day. And you are going to walk up through the gates toward a new beginning and a new life and a new celebration."

Dina, crying, asks, "Is Tony going to be okay?"

Debra answers, "You need to share with Tony that you will always love him and that you will never leave him. Your love will always be in his heart and his love for you will always be in your heart. That love will never leave you and it never dies. It is the one thing that continues and holds you two together."

Dina asks, "Is he going to be happy?"

Debra then says, "I feel like I have to do this." She gets off the healing table and kneels down in front of Dina. Debra says, "I know this is not me because I am still very dizzy. I am being told to do this. Hold my hands and know that this is God holding your hands. God says, 'Dina, I want you to repeat after me. God, I give you all my fear. I give you all my worry. I place all my control in your hands. I know you know what is best for me. And I know you know what is best for my husband. And when I give you this worry, I no longer hold on to this. I am free now.'" Debra cries as she says the words and Dina cries as she repeats the words. Sheri, standing behind Dina, also weeps.

Debra continues, "God says to you, 'When you give me the control, there are no more worries. There are no more fears. For you are one hundred percent in my hands and in my light and my glory and in my love.' From this point on, you have a light and it is radiating on the inside out. That is God."

Debra then says to Dina, "You couldn't have worn a more perfect shirt today." Dina is wearing a tie-dyed shirt with bright yellow, red, blue, green, and purple with a big smiley face right in the center of the shirt. "You have God inside you and outside of you and surrounding you. These days are going to be the best days because you are not going to feel worried anymore. God gave you the biggest gift because He said that your dad is going to come and he is going to walk with you and guide you."

With a little laugh of relief, Dina says, "I was hoping he would do this."

Debra adds, "It is like you are getting married, but you get to go to God's altar."

Dina says, "Yes, yes!"

Debra continues, "And it is a celebration and the angels are going to be singing and it is going to be beautiful and glorious and you are going to be so happy. You are going to be so happy." Dina is now smiling. Debra then says, "Your dad is being a smart aleck and he says, 'Do I have to show up in a suit?'"

Dina cracks up and everyone laughs along with her. The mood in the room is very light now and filled with joy. Dina says, "That sounds like him. He never wore suits."

Debra says, "Your dad is honored that God has allowed him to do this. He says, 'You will see me way before you are ready.' You will see your dad and you will know the time is close and you will say, 'I am not ready yet.' You will say that because you will still be hanging on for your husband. So what we are going to do right now is we are going to work on your heart. Your heart is connected to Tony's heart. We are going to give him healing and peace to know that if you're okay, he is okay. And if he is okay, then you are okay, and that is what we want, a healing of the heart.

"I hear these words: We are one in the spirit, we are one with the Lord. We are one in the spirit, we are one with the Lord. You and your husband are one in spirit and you are one with the Lord. So whether you are here or there, you are still one. And as long as you have the Lord, as long as he keeps the Lord within him, you will be one.

"You had a glimpse of seeing a little bit of the light, not all of it, 'because we don't want to ruin the celebration' is what I hear your dad say. It's like if we give it all to you now, then there is nothing for you to see later. He wants it to be exciting. Your dad wants this to be like you are walking into a party that you didn't know about and everyone says, 'Surprise!' That is what he is planning for you. There are going to be so many people that you have never met waiting there for you.

"I see a little baby. There is a little baby for you to see up there and you are going to be holding it. That is even going to be part of your mission; you are going to be holding babies. How exciting!"

Dina agrees. "Yes."

Debra says, "God gave us a gift today of not only allowing your father to come through, but for your mother to say a quick sorry. I think it was to mend things between you two. You will see her in a different light when you get there, when the time is right. But most importantly, He gave the gift of knowing how it is going to take place. Also, now you know that God watches and observes the transformation. So I want you to look at me right now lying on this table. This is you lying on this table. This is you lying in bed and there is this white light that goes right over me, like a shield." Debra lifts her arms just a little bit over her body to illustrate her words. "This right here, just above the body, is the spirit. The spirit comes out and it lifts and the body stays. So as the body becomes weaker, your spirit becomes stronger and you rise.

"So there will be times when your spirit will come in. There will be times when your spirit will go out. There will be times when you will be standing next to your husband, giving him support, while your body is here, until you are ready to leave. Then your dad will take you. Your dad will always be over here." Debra points to a space near the bed. "The beautiful thing is that God will observe and watch and if He thinks you are taking too much time, then you will be told it is time.

"You get extreme headaches, very strong headaches, and I am starting to get one now," Debra says.

Dina says, "I worry about that because last time I had a bad headache, I was nauseous with seizures."

Debra tells her, "When we get these headaches, we ask God to please take this headache away. 'I do not want it and I do not need it and I don't deserve it.' It gets intense in your temples. It gets extreme and it can take you down. So when that happens, remember that I said the spirit is above the body. If you remove the spirit, you remove the mind from the pain. You have to remove yourself. So when you do that you are saying, 'God, I remove myself from this pain.' You actually just did this now. You felt your head get a little pain and I asked you to say the words, and all of a sudden you didn't feel it anymore." Dina confirms this just happened. "When you do this, your spirit will not feel the pain, only your body will. You are learning that transition and you are learning how to do that. You are basically removing yourself from your body and then you don't feel the pain and it goes away. It might take a little bit to get there because you might be saying, 'I am still feeling this pain.' You need to say, 'God, please help me,' and God will help you. It's as if you are checking out. That is a tool that God is giving you.

"Remember how I gave you that vision that we were walking with God and then your dad came through? You weren't feeling anything in your body. You weren't really present." Dina nods in agreement. "You were completely present where we were on our journey. That is what we are doing. We are not going to be present where the pain is. We are going to be present right here." Debra gestures to the space right above her body. "You will still be in the room and you will still be able to hear, but you just won't be responding to your loved ones. And that is okay because this is what you will tell them: 'I will still hear you and all you need to know is that I love you and I won't be in pain if I am not responding.' When your family comes back in this room, I am supposed to explain this process to them. So now we place our hands on your head, allowing us to take out whatever is causing you this extreme pain in your head."

Sheri places her hands on both sides of Dina's head. She says, "The receptors are going crazy in there. We are just going to calm them down and soothe them and just allow you to feel at peace. What is beautiful is that God is giving you a tool to remove yourself from that pain. But know at all times when you remove yourself, this doesn't mean that you are leaving yet, it just means that you are not feeling the pain."

Debra says, "Remember that high-pitched sound I heard in my ear at the beginning? You are actually hearing better now than when you stepped into this room. You had to turn your head towards me for you to hear. I am now looking straight up and you are hearing more clearly." Dina says yes, confirming this. "So what is happening to you is that you are hearing more clearly. Your senses are all going to be heightened and accelerated. So let's say that it comes to a point where your eyes are closed and you can't really talk. All your other senses can hear and feel. Touch will be big for you, always touch. They always say that even if the mind goes, if the brain stops working, the heart still feels. The heart still knows. You don't have anything to fear because you are always going to know that our heart is our biggest voice, our biggest sense.

"God wants you to make sure that you know He made your hearing clearer and it is going to get clearer and clearer. You are going to say, 'Wow, I hear really well.' It is because your spirit hears it. Your ears don't need to hear it because your spirit does. This is going to be quite an interesting journey for you because you are going to start hearing, seeing, feeling in a different manner and in a higher vibration.

"Imagine light going through your entire being and white light is going through and touching every part of your body. That is God touching inside of you. What you voiced today, Dina, is what you put on God's platter. You put your worry. You put your fears. You voiced it and you gave it to God to hold. You are not in control and you do not need to worry about the control. You don't have one ounce of worry because all is well. All will be well. And you have a party to go to."

Dina smiles and laughs and says, "Yes, a big party at that!"

Debra asks, "Have you ever had that anticipation like, I have to get ready?" Dina is joyful and full of laughter. "A switch just turned on inside of you from being so frightened to kind of excited, and then you have your loved ones and feel like, I am sorry that I am so excited to go."

Dina says, "Yes."

Debra says, "I love the words that God said to you. You are one. You are one in spirit."

Dina says, "I can still be here."

Debra confirms, "God said you are one in the spirit; you are one in the Lord."

Dina expresses, "I just hope Tony is okay."

Debra says, "We are now going to bring Tony in." Sheri retrieves Tony from the waiting area. They are going to put Tony on the table and send him some healing energy. Tony lies on the table and Debra stands between him and Dina. Sheri starts sending healing energy at the top of Tony's head. Debra says, "Tony, the reason we brought you in is because Dina was shown how not to be in pain, what was going to happen, and that there was an exciting celebration waiting for her. She heard words from her dad. She released her fear to God, but she still has one more fear. That fear is that she needs to know that you are going to be okay." All three women are crying. "She loves you so much and she wants you to know that she is still going to be with you.

"God came into the room and He said, 'When two hearts become one, souls are one.' You will always be one in spirit and if you are one with the Lord, you will be connected. For the heart and the love never go away. It is the one thing, the one cord that will last from here to there and there to here, heaven and back. It is the vibration and the frequency that will never end. It is the one thing through which you can communicate. You can feel and you will never lose it. But she needs to know in her mind and in her soul that you are going to be okay. So we place this love and this healing and this strength into you, Tony." Sheri sends healing energy to Tony as Debra continues to speak.

"You know, Dina, when there is a loss, they have to grieve, they have to feel to heal. The love between the two of you is so grand. God will hold him in His light. Dina, your dad just said, 'How would you feel if you got to come back and tell Tony you were okay?'"

Dina says, "I would love it."

Debra asks Dina, "Do you like butterflies?" Dina laughs and says yes. Debra continues, "You get to pick the color and you get to pick the form and you bring that butterfly to your husband to let him know that you are okay. It is not you in the butterfly. It is just a symbol letting him know you are okay. The rest will be up to you while you are there, how you connect with him, but you can give him this sign right now.

"Tony needs to forever keep that shirt you are wearing, the tie-dyed shirt with a big smiley face in the middle. You will be his strength. He is your strength now but it will reverse. You will be his strength. But all will be well. Share with him the things that were said today–what is going to take place, how you are going to continue to hear and feel but you may not be able to speak. But he has to know that you are okay and we were able to do that in a practice here without us even knowing you were doing it. You were starting to get a headache and you were able to remove yourself from that pain."

Dina says, "Yes."

Debra says, "We didn't even know we did it until God told us that we did it. Then God gave you the tool to continue. Your husband worries about you being in pain, so you have to help him and explain to him the words that you heard today about how your spirit is not going to feel what the body does."

Dina says, "I am so relaxed right now."

Debra answers, "That's what we want, the peace within you. Just take that all in right now. You get to come back to this space again anytime when you feel panic or you feel the fear. We have to go back and remember what was said: Our heart is here and God is here, and remember you surrounded yourself with white light and now it is within you. It is God's control, and He said all is well and there is nothing for you to worry about, nothing. And I just loved how your dad was so comical." Dina laughs. "Don't be surprised if he comes in a white suit just to get your goat."

Dina, still laughing, says, "Tony will get a kick out of that one."

Sheri says, "The whole time he has been lying on the healing table, he has been receiving strength and balance as I have been placing energy up and down his body. I feel like Tony and Dina need to hold hands."

"I have something to say," adds Debra. "And these are not my words. These are words for the two of you. I want you each, both of you, to reverse your roles. Tony, it is you lying in the hospital bed and Dina, you are sitting next to him. I want you to feel what you would want for one another. And I can feel your husband feeling, *I want her to be at peace.* And I can feel Dina wanting him to be at peace."

Tony says, "That is for sure." Dina smiles and laughs.

Debra goes on, "I want you to hold hands rather than feel worry for one another. We place that worry in God's hands and we let God take control of the situation, knowing that He knows what is best, knowing that He knows the timing. He knows the process. No matter what the body goes through, remember that the spirit does not feel. As long as you two are holding hands, both of your hearts will feel the peace. That is what we will do from this day forward, is not have the worry. Not have the fear. Only hold each other's hands, one giving the other the peace that each wants.

"You fulfill him with the peace and the light that is within you and he will breathe and give you the energy of peace and love that he has for you. That is what the hands do, and what the heart does is it connects and it receives. You will both vibrate at the same frequency of peace and love."

Dina says, "We always have."

Debra says, "And that is the gift that you two both hold. As long as you know this, it doesn't have to come through words. It doesn't have to come through the eyes. It comes through the vibration of touch and through the hands. He knows that you will be feeling it no matter where you are or what state you are, and you know he will be feeling it. If you both know that you are at peace and that you feel complete love, you both know that you are both going to be fine."

Dina says, "Yes."

Debra says, "God will hold you in that peace and love and that light. Let it be something beautiful that both of you will never forget, but that when you meet again you can talk about it. You will share it with those on the other side and he can share it with those who are here."

Dina smiles and laughs some more. She says, "I definitely feel at peace after coming here."

Debra says to Dina, "We don't always know the whys, but we are content and we have no fear and we feel calm. We know that God knows the whys and that He knows what is best for us, so we can be okay with everything."

Sheri leaves the room and returns with Dina's sisters. Everyone circles around Dina and holds hands to pray. Debra says, "We want to give thanks to God for allowing Sheri and me to be the instruments for this healing. And for giving us the tools, the messages, the vibrations, and the love we all felt. We give thanks for the words that came through to show us what is waiting. To show us what is coming, to show us how to handle it, to show us how to walk through it gracefully, but more importantly, to be at peace through it all. We give thanks to God for bringing through your father and your mom."

Dina says, "And my doggie!"

Debra continues, "We are grateful that your dad's personality came through." Dina laughs and wears a big smile. "God gave you a glimpse, and what a beautiful vision He gave to you."

Dina says to everyone, "It is going to be a big ol' party!"

Debra says, "We give thanks to you, Dina, and to your loved ones for being here. We are now going to end this healing with the Lord's Prayer." They recite the Lord's Prayer together and there is not a dry eye in the room.

❧    ❧    ❧

When Dina was in her healing session, Tony was concerned that she would be sitting too long and would be in pain from not having her medicine. Dina told Tony after the session that she had not been in any pain during the entire session and felt at peace.

Dina's sister Lisa called Sheri on July 10, 2014, to tell her that Dina had passed.

Tony shared this message with Debra and Sheri: "As Dina was ready to pass, her final words were, 'Okay, Dad, okay, Dad.'"

Two days after her passing, Tony received a butterfly key ring and a butterfly music box in the mail from Dina.

## Words from God

The process of dying, it is God's process. You don't need to worry, or take on, or assist. You need to know that your loved ones will never die alone for I never leave any one of my children. And I am always there in times of need. Do not hold guilt. Do not hold shame. Do not hold responsibility. You have enough on your plate. Do only what you can do. Do not do any more, and trust that it will all happen the way I want it to. And if you try to control it, it is still not going to work out your way. It is going to work out my way, which will be fine. If you trust that it will work out my way, then it frees you from worrying how it should turn out. And that is what I am here to do, to free you from this worry. Pray with me, not to me. Pray with me.am always there. I am on your journey. I am listening and watching you. Trust the process of what's happening in your life, for everything is happening for you to become who you need to be for this next step in your journey.

# CHAPTER NINETEEN
# LOVE NEVER DIES

## Tina Nelson Healing Session
## September 23, 2014

Tina was a third grade schoolteacher for thirty years. Tina came in for a healing because of guilt associated with decisions made years earlier when her brother was taken off life support after an accident.

The night before her brother passed, Tina had a vivid dream that he had been killed in an accident. She told her boyfriend the next morning and he told her to get ready for work and call him later. That night she received a call from the hospital that her brother had been in an accident. She felt haunted because she was given a warning and never shared it with her brother. All these years later she still dealt with a tremendous amount of guilt.

Her brother's passing gave her years of pain. During the healing session she was taken on a spiritual journey with God in which she was taken to the veil where she was greeted by her brother. She was not only given words of peace, she was shown and felt this peace within her soul.

The Healing Session
Debra begins, "I feel this warmth that is encompassing my chest area. That is God's love. He is holding you and giving you this love. Because Tina, you have felt unloved and God just wants you to feel loved right now. It is what you need and

it is the embrace of love. You are always so sweet and always having pure intentions and a pure heart with everyone who comes around you. It is time for you to receive this love that you deserve because you give so much love. I feel a lot of pressure going into my forehead to the point that I can almost not stand the pain. It's heavy and it is going right into your third eye.

"They are opening and fine-tuning you to this spirit world and to God. Things will become clearer for you. But I feel this heaviness in my head. It is like a weight and it so heavy. This is the weight that you hold. You keep holding on to this heaviness. It is within your mind. The control is within your mind. So God is going into your third eye and He is releasing and taking away everything that is preventing your mind from receiving all that you deserve. When that happens..." Debra takes a deep breath as the pain in her head reaches an almost unbearable intensity. "I want you to tell God these words and repeat after me quietly in your mind. 'Allow my mind to be at peace, Lord. I give the control to you, releasing all that my mind is holding on to.' You don't even realize what you are doing. ' It's like you have done this work, but the mind is blocking it. So if we can remove the control of the mind, then you will see everything release and calibrate through the body.

"Tina, we are now going to take a spiritual journey. We are removing the control of the mind. What we are going to do now, Tina, is let go of the control; this means we are not thinking. We are not thinking about what is going to happen next. We are letting the control go and letting it be what it will be. There you go, Tina, you did a good job and I just felt your spirit release. I just felt it lift and I just felt you relax your whole body. I feel a coolness surround my whole body. I feel this coolness as if someone is coming into the room. I can feel a strong, strong presence." Debra's voice becomes soft as she says, "I feel like crying because it is God. Oh my, this is overwhelming." She is crying. "God is standing on the left side of the healing table by your feet. He is walking forward. Imagine the vision that you have of God in His robe. You are His child and He has come to embrace you and to hold you.

"So as He leans over, He picks your spirit up, and you are standing in front of Him and He has His arms around you so strong. He says, 'It is okay to cry now because I have you. I am holding you and I will keep you safe.' And you just feel like finally, someone is holding you." Tina, Sheri, and Debra are all crying. "Someone you trust. Someone who you know loves you unconditionally and there are no conditions for this hug. There is no reason why you have to give back. He just holds you and He says, 'I want to take your pain away. Please allow me to take your pain away.' He continues to hold you and He is not going to let you go. That's how much He loves you. Even if you tried to get out of that embrace, you are not moving. Now He stands and He puts His arms around your shoulders and He turns you. It no longer feels like we are in this room. It feels like we are in this space that is so full of love. You see nothing but white. There is nothing else around but white. You are both looking forward and you are just standing in that space where you are feeling peace."

Debra continues, speaking God's words. "What you are seeing is my kingdom. What lies beyond that light is heaven. I am giving you peace and love that comes from there. As I stand here holding you tight, I am not going to let you fall. It may feel like you are going to fall to your knees, but I won't let you, for I am going to bring your brother forth. He is going to walk through that white light, closer and closer to you. Now you can see him from a distance"–Debra is crying as she sees him—"and now he is coming forward. You can see him and you want to fall to your knees. You are saying, 'I just wanted this last time. I just wanted to be here with you.' I know you want to be here in heaven with him, but it is not your time. So

I bring you here for this moment to be where you wanted to be."

Debra continues in her own voice, "He is coming closer and closer and you almost want to collapse because it is so emotional. Now he stands in front of you. It is as if God is reuniting both of you. Now you feel so much peace, and this calm just came through me, like all of a sudden I feel so strong because I am looking at him. I have this strength that I never thought I would have. You are looking him up and down and all around. He even spins his body around and says, 'See, I am whole.' Now he is going to embrace you. Hold him, hug him, kiss him, and smell him." Tina has tears rolling down her cheeks. "And your brother looks at you and he says, 'Shhh, you don't need to tell me. I already know. I already know. I can hear you, I can see you, and I can feel you. I am here now to embrace you and to show you and to love you. I am here to thank you.'" Tina looks confused and it is clear that she doesn't understand why her brother would offer her thanks.

Debra explains, "God looks at your brother and nods. He nods, like, Go ahead and continue. Your brother says, 'I am here to thank you for always loving me. The pain that you hold is because of love. I am here to honor you for that love that you have always held. I am really sorry that my love has caused you so much pain. We love each other so much, but it should not cause you pain. God didn't give us love so that we would be in pain. He gave us that pain so we knew how much we loved. And I love you and I honor you for loving me. That is something that will never end.'

"God is nodding because that is the meaning of love. We now have found the root of the pain that is in your heart. We are now going to release this root so that you can be in peace and comfort, knowing that you are one with your brother right now. Your brother now wants to take you somewhere to show you something. You are going to walk with your brother and God is walking behind you. He is taking you towards the light. You are taking each step very slowly and you are thinking, *What am I going to see? What is he going to show me?* Your brother has the biggest smile on his face and says, 'If you only knew.'

"He is so honored to take you here. This is an honor beyond honor that you get to go to this space. Now we are getting really close to this veil and God says, 'Stop.' As you stand right there at the veil, God says, 'Listen, for the angels are singing and they are rejoicing your name. For this is your kingdom and they are honoring you.' Hear the angels praising you. It is beautiful, it is a higher pitch than we have ever heard before. You are just surrounded in this light but you can hear the music beyond that light, beyond that veil. They are singing and rejoicing for you and for who you are. It is so beautiful. God has His arms spread out, taking in this light, this love, and this rejoicing. He is putting His arms up and saying, 'Rejoice, rejoice. Take it in, take the words in, rejoice.'"

Debra continues, "Feel the renewed you. You look at your brother with the biggest smile, and you are fine now and you're not crying. You are smiling. You both hold hands and lean back and spin around in a circle as if to dance and you are both so happy. Your brother says, 'This is what it will be like. I will be waiting with God when it is your time. I will greet you and I will be the one to walk you into this light where they are rejoicing your name. But the colors, the visions, the children, and all those waiting to greet you, I get to show you to them. I get to show off my sister. I get to be the one to say, She is here. She has arrived. It will be a beautiful moment, but until then you need to rejoice on Earth as it is in heaven. For you can have all that is yours and more on Earth. Be loved, feel loved, and feel my love, stand in it. As you stand in this white light, God is infusing you from heaven from your head to your toes. This light is going through you like a beam of light, touching every part of you. This light is cleansing you and renewing you and it is going inside you to give you strength, to give you peace, to give you comfort, to give you everything you need here on Earth while you complete your journey.'

"God says, 'One more embrace from your brother and he has to go back. I want you to embrace him and feel him and hold him tight.' You do just that, and you feel this comfort and it just feels so good. You are not letting him go because it feels so good. He kisses you on the cheek, and he has this big, lopsided grin. He says, 'It is going to be awesome. Your life there and your life here, it is going to be awesome. I am proud of you, sis, and I love you.' As he walks away, he throws you a kiss." Both Tina and Sheri are crying at the power of this moment.

"God comes and He puts His arms around you and He walks you back to that space where we are standing together, and He says, 'Today is your day. You have been rebirthed. You have been given a new start, a new beginning. I gave you a piece of heaven. Continue to stand in it and feel it and love it. Know that it is never going to leave you and neither am I. With that, you have no more hurt. No more questions. No more worry, for everything that now comes to you is going to become clearer because we have opened up your aware-ness. You have been rebirthed into this new love and peace. Tonight will be the first time that you sleep not in pain, but in total comfort. I will be watching you. You may even cry a little. Know that my arm will be around you, consoling you, and as you sleep you will feel my presence. You can feel my presence from this day forward. Go, my child.'" Tina's spirit goes back into her body. "'Remember what just happened. Remember the gift I gave you. I gave you a piece of heaven. I surrounded you inside and out with my love. When I say go, my child, I am saying, Continue this journey, your purpose with me. Remember the smile on your brother's face.'"

Debra continues, "As you come back in the room, God steps away. You can feel Him lifting out of the room. Whenever you go to that space of pain, remind yourself, 'I cannot go back to that space because not only am I letting my brother down, not only am I letting myself down, I am letting God down. No more. I am free and lifted from all pain and all worry.' Allow that energy to flow through you and around you. Others will see this shift around you as well. They will see God's light shining through you."

❧ ❧ ❧

The healing session ended with the women holding hands and reciting the Lord's Prayer. Tina said that now she felt so free. She had held guilt about her brother's passing for so many years, and it was God's assurances that allowed her to finally release all the guilt and pain she had carried.

# Chapter Twenty

# Analysis of Debra Martin's & Sheri Getten's Brainwaves During Healing Sessions

August 18, 2014
By Karen Newell, co-founder of Sacred Acoustics

I first began measuring brainwave activity to determine how sound frequencies affect the brain when in altered states of awareness. The main purpose has been to determine what brainwave states people attain when in these altered states so that we may then create sets of audio frequencies that will help others to attain similar states of expanded consciousness. In this context, we have collected data from many subjects in many states of brainwave activity.

The brain has several levels of electrical output, as follows:

**Delta (0-4 Hz)** These frequencies appear in deep sleep, unconsciousness, and meditative trance.

**Theta (4-8 Hz)** This brain state is associated with enhanced intuition, creativity, fantasies, imagery, and dreams. These brainwaves are most pronounced during meditation, prayer, and spiritual awareness.

**Alpha (8-12 Hz)** Alpha brainwaves are a reflection of mental focus, contemplation, calm, and relaxation. It seems to be a bridge from the conscious to the unconscious when a person is alert but not actively processing information.

**Beta (12-30 Hz)** This state corresponds to the active state of adults who are engaged in conversation, physical activities, solving problems, and analyzing and processing information.

**Gamma (above 30 Hz)** Frequencies at this level are found in individuals at moments of profound insight and levels of high sensory information processing.

Our primary measurement tool has been an IBVA/BlueVAS device used specifically to measure brainwave activity. The IBVA probes are attached to the forehead, measuring the frontal lobes of both the right and left brain. The device software displays real-time electrical output from each side of the brain as well as coherence between the left and right brain.

I had the opportunity to gather brainwave data during several healing sessions in 2014 from both Debra Martin and Sheri Getten. During some sessions, the device was attached to both Debra and Sheri, measuring each of their right and left frontal lobes simultaneously. Baseline readings were taken from both Debra and Sheri in order to determine their resting brainwave states. All verbal comments and discussion were also recorded to match up with the brainwave data for later analysis.

Compared to their resting states, Debra and Sheri each displayed some notable brainwave activity during healing sessions. While making connection to Spirit and performing spiritual surgery, Debra maintained a rather strong delta/theta state (0-8Hz) and less strong alpha state (8-12Hz). During some periods, she also showed simultaneous peaks in the gamma range (50+ Hz) while the beta range (12-30Hz) stayed in a relatively quiet state. Interestingly, much of the time, no matter what state the brain was in, the left and right brain were identical to each other, a state known as high coherence.

Sheri maintained a strong delta state during most of each healing session, sometimes moving into the theta/alpha ranges. She also showed simultaneous peaks in the gamma range, maintaining delta and gamma states at the same time. Like Debra, there were periods when Sheri's left and right brain were coherent with each other. Sheri's brain also remained relatively quiet in the beta range. Remarkably, Sheri remained standing during the healing sessions, often moving around the table. Typically, this type of activity would produce higher measurements in the beta range.

The IBVA software can also show coherence between both Debra's and Sheri's brains. There was some evidence of their brains being somewhat close to coherent with each other (remarkable in itself), but not nearly as strong as the coherence seen between each of their individual left and right brain.

Much research has demonstrated that individuals often attain theta brainwave states through meditation and altered states of consciousness. Less often, delta and gamma are prominent in these same states. My personal observation of brainwave states corresponds with these trends. Both Debra and Sheri display a higher-than-normal level of delta and gamma ranges while in the healing session process.

What struck me as most significant is the state of coherency in both Debra and Sheri that was apparent while performing a healing session. This is something I personally have witnessed as quite rare during any level of activity. It is something I have been quite attuned to and looking for because binaural beats, a component of the audio technology produced by Sacred Acoustics, has been reported to drive the listener into a state of coherency, where the left and right brain activity corresponds completely.

At this time, I have not personally witnessed coherence in any person's frontal lobes while listening to many forms of binaural beat technology. What we often see is decreased activity in the left frontal lobe and increased activity in the right frontal lobe, although this varies widely between individuals. Debra and Sheri seem to naturally and effortlessly enter this state while performing their healing sessions. Further study involving other areas of the brain would confirm how fully their coherence can be measured.

# CHAPTER TWENTY-ONE
# LIGHT YOUR CANDLE WITHIN

At the end of every healing session, Debra and Sheri encourage each person to light his or her own candle within. It is up to you now to have your own direct connect with God. You are a part of your own healing process. The most important thing we can do for ourselves is to take the time out and connect with God.

When you step aside and allow God to enter, a shift occurs within. We are all so powerful beyond anything we can imagine, but do we ever just sit down and take the time to listen? We busy ourselves with our children, our work, and our cell phones. We have stopped listening to the voice within us and sought outward advice. We search the internet, ask our friends, and consult our cell phones for answers. All we need to do is just sit and ask God and listen for the answer. The answers are always there for us. God knows us better than anybody else and always has our highest and best interest at heart. He is our backbone, He is our strength, and He wants nothing more than for us to take His hand and walk with Him.

The number one priority in our busy lives should be to take this time out for ourselves and connect with God. It is so simple, yet so powerful, and it could transform your life. Take time out of your day to pray and connect with God. Spend less time worrying and more time listening.

When you light your candle, it is very symbolic. You are lighting your candle within. The more you light your candle, the brighter your own light becomes. Even if you don't receive or hear anything, it doesn't matter. What matters is that you are taking the time to go within and connect to your source. Stilling your mind helps you to keep balance in your life. It is the still, small voice within us that always knows the truth about any situation we might come across. Get to know this voice, get to know this stillness. It is your own personal lighthouse guiding you on your path and keeping you safe. Sometimes answers don't always come to us in that moment of silence, but they will come, probably when you least expect it.

This devotion of lighting our candle and connecting to God will bring us the peace, joy, and love that are needed to have a balanced life. It is the time to communicate and pour your heart out to your Lord God. Some days you may want to sit in silence and some days you may want to pray. Some days you will do both. There is no right or wrong way; it is all up to you. If it were too complicated, then no one would take the time to silence their minds. Play with it, have fun with it, enjoy it, and make it your own.

This is your connection with God, and no one's is the same. Find a time that works for you, as not every day will be the same. What will be the same is that you will always look forward to this "me" time because you are carving time out for yourself. You are important and you play an important role in many people's lives. It is like an instrument; if you only pick it up and play every now and then, you won't be very good at it. If you take time every day, every week, then you get better and better. You become more successful when you take time every day to fine-tune your instrument, and this instrument is you.

Do you not want to be the best you can be at all times? Even when things are crazy in your outside world, you can always find calm in your inside world. When your inside world is calm, you can handle any situation that comes your way because of the calm that surrounds you. There will always be bumps and sharp curves on the road ahead of us, but when we are balanced we are better equipped for these challenges. Just remember that there is nothing too big for God. Build a relationship with Him even though we may not understand why these difficult challenges are happening in our lives. Know that God is walking you through it, and with that trust you will get through any situation.

When you are on the wrong path, He is always there to pick you up and carry your load. We were never intended to carry this heavy load on our own. God wants to lighten our loads so that we may be free to do the work we were intended to do. No load is too big for God. It is we who carry the shame and guilt of this load. There are always going to be hurdles on our paths. What we do when we come across these hurdles is key. We sometimes make these hurdles bigger than they actually are and allow them to block us and hold us back. When you live a life of connectedness to God, then you become aware of these hurdles and know that they are just bumps in the road. When you open up and allow God to do His work in your life, then you will no longer fear these hurdles. Stay in faith, stay in prayer, stay in communication with the Lord, and allow Him to hold your hand during these trying times. It is so much easier than doing this walk alone!

Walking with God through these tests is what gives us faith. When we have faith and trust in our lives, then no obstacle is too big. Take this lesson, learn from it, and walk forward knowing God is guiding you every step of the way. Sometimes we get stuck in our lives where it is very painful to move forward. Don't ever fear change, for change means another door is opening. Don't feel that change means that it is frightening. Look at it as a beautiful light being shined upon you. Do not fear and stay stuck where you are; instead, look at it as from this point on, another door is being opened and it will bring you closer to your purpose here on Earth.

When we get to a point in our lives where we know we have to make a change but we don't know how to make that change, we need to light our candle within and pray to God:

"Guide me. I trust that you will guide me and trust that you will close the doors that need to be closed and I trust that you will open the doors that need to be opened. I will not fear walking forward for I know you are in front of me, knowing what is best for me on all levels, leading me to where I need to be in order to serve my purpose on Earth." And sometimes people will ask, "How do I know that it is the right door to go through?" And God answers, "If it's not and you are praying to me and lighting your candle, the door would not be open."

Allow Him to control your path. By doing that, it frees you from worry. You will start to build a relationship with God and trust in Him. This does not happen overnight and you must have discipline and desire to connect every day. Lighting your candle then becomes something that you look forward to every day. It will become the most important part of your day.

May the light of God always shine upon you.
May the love of God always be with you.
May you seek God's help and grace on this path of life.
May you ask for God's help to take away all burdens on your path.
May you never forget where you came from.
Try not to judge those around you for you may not understand their lessons in life.
Only focus upon yourself and brightening the light within you.
It is time to take charge to heal yourself within.
Be the light that people gather towards and want to be around.
Take this time to be alone in meditation.
We never know how much time we have on Earth.
Use it wisely and use it to get to know the God within you.
Go within or go without.

Thank you for reading our book. Our intent is that all who read this book will receive some level of healing or simply feel the love of God. We believe when one is healed, we are all healed.

# ABOUT THE AUTHORS

Debra is a research medium certified by the University of Arizona and is currently a Level 5 Certified Research Medium at the Windbridge Institute for Applied Research in Human Potential (www.windbridge.org). She is also author of *Believe Beyond Seeing*, which details her connections as a medium with the afterlife; and the children's book *Me and My Angels*. Debra has been featured in national media including A&E's documentary *Mediums: We See Dead People* and appeared in various news reports. One report, "The Medium Who Solved a Murder," was broadcast by the Phoenix, Arizona, CBS network affiliate and gained national attention. Debra is the mother of four children and resides in Scottsdale, Arizona.

Sheri's journey to becoming a healer started after she began having visions and dreams that healing people around the world was her life's calling. This led her to earn a Level III Reconnective Healing Practitioner certification. Reconnective healing is often a life-changing experience, utilizing new frequencies to allow for the healing of body, mind, and spirit. Since that initial training, Sheri has developed her own unique technique. Sheri is the mother of four children and resides in Scottsdale, Arizona.

Debra Martin and Sheri Getten have been collaborating for more than nineteen years on their spiritual journey. They are now bringing healing and spiritual awakening to people all over the world. By combining their gifts, the two have a more profound effect than they could have working individually.

They connect the present with the Spirit world and open new levels of consciousness to a wider reality where healing can take place. Debra and Sheri are able to bring a piece of heaven into each one of their healing sessions. They give each person a direct message from God.

Debra and Sheri were both ordained as healing ministers at The Logos Center in Scottsdale, Arizona, on November 19, 2013.

Website: www.debraandsheri.com
Facebook: www.facebook.com/debraandsheri
Twitter: www.twitter.com/DebraandSheri

We encourage you to take the time to light your candle within and have your own "Direct Connect to God." We were given a vision from God to create a candle that would go hand in hand with our book. You can purchase your own candle from our website:
www.debraandsheri.com

Made in the USA
Middletown, DE
12 April 2015